BELLE OF THE WEST

The True Story of Belle Starr

BELLE OF THE WEST
The True Story of Belle Starr

Margaret Rau

MORGAN
REYNOLDS
Incorporated

620 South Elm Street Suite 384
Greensboro, North Carolina 27406
http://www.morganreynolds.com

BELLE OF THE WEST: THE TRUE STORY OF BELLE STARR

Copyright © 2001 by Margaret Rau

Picture credits: Courtesy of the Oklahoma Historical Society

Library of Congress Cataloging-in-Publication Data

Rau, Margaret.
     Belle of the West: the true story of Belle Starr / Margaret Rau.
        p.cm.
     Includes bibliographical references (p.) and index.
     ISBN 1-883846-68-4 (lib. bdg. : alk. paper)
       1. Starr, Belle, 1848-1889. 2. Women outlaws--West (U.S)--Biography. 3.
     Outlaws--West (U.S.)--Biography. 4. West (U.S.)--Biography. 5. Frontier and pioneer
     life--West (U.S.) I.Title.

     F594.S8 R38 2001
     364.1'55'092--dc21
     [B]

                                                                         00-053497

Printed in the United States of America
First Edition

Contents

Belle Starr, May 23, 1886. *(Photo by Roeder, Fort Smith, Arkansas. Courtesy of the Archives & Manuscripts Division of the Oklahoma Historical Society, 1356.)*

Prologue

BELLE STARR: BANDIT QUEEN

The name Belle Starr conjures images of stage coach robberies, smoking six-shooters, and bar room brawls, but the reputation of the most well-known female outlaw of the Old West is based more on rumor and hearsay than any tangible evidence. A dime novel published in 1889 after her death by Richard K. Fox, *Belle Starr: The Bandit Queen, or the Female Jesse James*, was widely read in the United States and abroad. The book told many tall tales about Belle, claiming that she was the beautiful and ruthless leader of a band of outlaws. In truth, Belle was never convicted of any more serious crimes than horse theft. It was her marriages to and friendships with various outlaws, such as the James brothers, that caused tongues to wag. Eventually, the gossip turned to legend, and these spectacular tales would forever secure her infamous place in the colorful history of the Old West.

Here is the true story of Belle Starr, which begins in a frontier town with a little girl named Myra Maybelle.

Chapter One

A GIRL NAMED MYRA MAYBELLE

In later years, she came to be known as Belle Starr, the Bandit Queen of Texas. But few would have guessed that such a future awaited the sprightly dark-haired girl of ten whom everyone in Carthage knew as Myra Maybelle Shirley. People laughed good-humoredly whenever she went galloping pell-mell down Carthage's Main Street, at intervals popping off bullets from the huge pistol she carried.

Such behavior would not have been tolerated on the main streets of old Southern towns. But Carthage was a frontier town, the county seat of Jasper County in southeast Missouri. It was a town of some 300 inhabitants, mostly immigrants from Southern states. The architecture resembled that of many Southern towns. The main street was lined with shade trees and brick business buildings, among which stood a two-story courthouse and an adjacent jail.

Myra Maybelle's behavior was treated with a certain

amount of tolerance by the townsfolk because her father, John Shirley, was the town's most prominent citizen and the wealthiest man around. A member of the influential Shirley family of Virginia and Kentucky, John Shirley roamed around a bit in his youth, earning himself the title of the family black sheep. He had married three times and divorced twice. He had two children, a boy and a girl, by his first wife and none by his second. His third wife, Elizabeth, or Eliza as she was commonly called, was a teenager at the time of their marriage. She was part Cherokee and a member of the Hatfield clan, famous for its bloody feud with the McCoys.

Eliza and John eventually migrated to Missouri, where they began homesteading a 600-acre farm on the rolling foothills of the Ozarks. Eliza's first three children were born on the farm. There was John Allison, nicknamed Bud, and Myra Maybelle, who was born six years later on February 5, 1848 according to her tombstone. Edwin was born a year later. When Myra Maybelle was about two years old, John Shirley sold the farm and bought two large lots in Carthage, where he built a hotel, probably of brick to match the town's architecture.

Most frontier hotels were crude buildings, often little more than shacks. Pads spread on a dirt floor provided sleeping quarters. Wash-ups consisted of a battered tin pan of cold water, a ragged wash cloth, and a grimy towel. Soap was a luxury.

John and Eliza were determined to have a hotel worthy

of the Shirley name. Their's provided separate bedrooms for the guests, comfortable beds, and clean sheets and blankets. Visitors tired and grimy from a long trek could expect a real bath in a tub filled with hot water.

Two young slaves helped the Shirleys with their chores. One, a livery boy, took care of the horses, mules, and oxen of the travelers who stopped there. The other, a young girl, helped Eliza with the housework and cooking.

Eliza prepared sumptuous meals for her guests, giving them a touch of Southern cooking. And she served the meals on a table covered with fresh white linen and set with real silver. After the evening meal, the little maid served choice liqueurs in the drawing room while Eliza entertained the guests with a piano concert. Considered a necessity in every well-to-do Southern home, the piano was brought to the frontier town at great expense. The Shirley hotel did not lack customers as its fame quickly spread up and down the trail. The hotel's success, along with other wise investments John Shirley made, was responsible for his wealth.

Like most Southern parents with means, the Shirleys wanted their daughter to have the advantages of a good education. Since there were no female academies in Carthage, John Shirley enlisted the aid of other wealthy families to open one, and in 1855, the brand new Carthage Female Academy was ready to accept pupils. Myra Maybelle, a bright-eyed girl of seven or eight, attended the school along with other daughters from the richest families in Jasper County. The girls studied reading, spelling, grammar, arithmetic, deportment, Latin, Greek, and Hebrew. Myra Maybelle's father paid an extra fee for his daughter to take piano lessons. No Southern girl was considered cultured unless she could play the piano.

By age ten, Myra Maybelle was supplementing her education at the academy with classes at the regular town school, which she attended with the two older boys. By this time, two more boys had been added to the Shirley family. The youngest was still just a baby.

One of Myra's classmates recalls her as a vivacious girl, small for her age, and olive complexioned like her mother. According to her, Myra Maybelle had one chief fault. She could never back down from a quarrel with anyone, boy or girl, even if it turned into a physical fight. Otherwise, Myra's classmate concluded, "she seemed a nice little girl. In fact the whole entire Shirley family were nice people."

But her classmate also recalled that Myra Maybelle liked to show off her status as the daughter of the renowned hotel owner and the richest little girl in Carthage. Myra Maybelle was the center of attention at the hotel. Her quick mind and sprightly manner made her a favorite among the guests. They often asked her to perform for them on the piano, and she was quick to oblige, pleased by the high praise she received for her skills. It was never long before the guests discovered Myra Maybelle's weak spot: her quick temper. They would tease her until she exploded, sending her tormentors into gales of laughter. Then, to appease her, they would lavish gifts on the little girl until she was thoroughly spoiled.

But Myra Maybelle's life had another side. She spent hours with her two passions: horses and her brother Bud, whom she adored. She could ride the most skittish of horses, and her love for them lasted until her death. Often brother and sister took long, rambling horseback rides together, galloping past the farms of the settlers and into the thickly wooded Ozarks. It was during these times that Bud, an expert marksman with pistol and rifle, taught his sister how to shoot. And it was his wild laughter that egged her on when she made those pistol-popping rides down the town's main street.

The people of Carthage had more to worry about than Myra Maybelle's childish antics. The 1840s and '50s were years of tension for Missourians. The state was almost equally divided between immigrants from the Northeast, who settled in northern Missouri, and those coming from the South, who settled in southern Missouri. Most of the people in northern Missouri were opposed to slavery. Those who settled in southern Missouri, whether they owned slaves or not, were intensely loyal to the South.

Nowhere was the situation as intense as it was along the southeast border of Missouri, and especially in Jasper County, which shared its boundary with the free state of Kansas to the west. For years, relations between Jasper

County and Kansas had been bad. Bands of Jayhawkers from Kansas frequently crossed the border to make raids in Jasper County, while bands of Bushwhackers from Missouri reciprocated by crossing the border to raid Kansas farms.

In 1855, relations between the two states exploded when John Brown, an ardent abolitionist, learned that the South was actively sponsoring loyal citizens to migrate to Kansas, hoping that their increasing numbers would change the state to a pro-slavery, pro-South one. Brown traveled posthaste to Kansas. In July, he led a small raiding party of Kansas abolitionists into Missouri. There they attacked several farm houses. Though the people who lived in them owned no slaves themselves, they were solidly pro-South, so Brown and his followers rounded up all the adult males and executed them.

Infuriated Southerners responded by crossing the border and burning down the abolitionist town of Lawrence, from which the Kansas raiders had come. Three months later they returned to burn down John Brown's house.

After stirring things up in Kansas and Missouri, Brown carried his campaign to Harper's Ferry, West Virginia, where he tried to take over the Union arsenal there. He was captured and hanged after a brief trial. Following his death, his name became the rallying cry of abolitionists everywhere. Meanwhile, many Southerners were becoming equally strident in their support of slavery. In Carthage, the most outspoken advocates for the South were John

Shirley and his son Bud. Myra Maybelle was quick to echo her father and brother's fiery opinions.

In December of 1860, as Myra neared her thirteenth birthday, events in the East were rising to a climax that would change the course of many lives, both in the North and the South. Abraham Lincoln had just been elected president of the United States, although there had been a growing demand by Southern states for secession from the Union if he were elected president. Following Lincoln's forthright message to Congress that month warning against secession, South Carolina immediately responded by seceding from the Union. Mississippi, Florida, Alabama, Louisiana, Georgia, and Texas quickly followed South Carolina.

Excitement ran high in Carthage at the news. The Shirley family was pro-Confederate, and no one was more stirred by it than Bud Shirley, now a young man in his twenties. He began speaking openly of putting words into action and joining the bands of guerrillas already roaming around the countryside to harass Union soldiers stationed there, as well as abolitionists and pro-North farmers.

Then on April 12, 1861, Union guns at Fort Sumter on the South Carolina coast returned fire on a threatening Southern fleet massing in the harbor. The surrender of the fort to the new confederacy was only days away.

There was no holding Bud back now. He cleaned and primed his pistols. He had his horse newly shod and groomed and his boots shined. Then off he rode down Carthage's Main Street, leading a few ardent followers. They planned to form their own guerrilla band and drive all Yankees out of Jasper County.

Almost everyone in Carthage turned out to give Bud and his companions a hero's farewell. Thirteen-year-old Myra Maybelle's eyes glowed as she watched her brother ride off, a slender young man with a shock of hair as black as Myra's and the same flashing black eyes. As he passed, Myra's voice rose above the clatter of horses' hooves and the clamor of the crowd, vowing to devote her whole life and energies to helping her brother in his great mission.

Chapter Two

DEATH OF A GUERRILLA

The proclamation of war that followed the firing on Fort Sumter divided Missouri. Even Governor Claiborne F. Jackson, who had earlier announced a policy of neutrality, now showed his real loyalties by boldly declaring his Southern allegiance. Missouri became a free-for-all state. Northern guerrillas and Southern guerrillas began forming small bands to burn and loot the homes and farms of sympathizers on opposing sides.

The leader of the largest number of Southern guerrillas was a man named William C. Quantrill. The bands under Quantrill's command included such future outlaws as Frank and Jesse James and the Younger brothers. Throughout the war years, Quantrill and his men were so violent and the havoc they wrought was so great that Northerners looked on him as a bloodthirsty monster, while Southerners praised him as a patriot and hero.

Bud Shirley and his band of followers had also become a threat to Northern sympathizers and the Union troops stationed in Jasper County. Many efforts were made to capture Shirley, the captain of the band. Yet Bud continued to evade every attempt, like a shadow slipping in and out of the nets Union forces spread for him. He even continued to make frequent visits to his family in Carthage, entering the town and slipping out again before Union soldiers could get to him.

Much of Bud's success in evading his enemies was due to his sister, Myra Maybelle, who was now well into her teens. No longer the sprightly little girl popping her pistol up and down Main Street, she was developing into a young lady with a creamy complexion, sparkling black eyes, and long dark hair. Heads turned to watch her whenever she rode by on her spirited horse, sitting straight as an arrow, seldom firing her pistol, though she always carried it proudly with her. In later years, she was to refer to it affectionately as "my baby."

Young and innocent-looking, the daring teenager slipped in and out of enemy camps, gathering information for her

Bud Shirley fought with a band of Southern guerrillas led by this man, William C. Quantrill.

brother. Flirting with Union soldiers, she used her wiles to worm important information out of them. It might be the route of an enemy ammunition train or the number of Union soldiers camped in one spot, or perhaps some new camp that Union forces had secretly set up to surprise Bud and his band. Most important, Myra Maybelle was often able to learn about secret traps set for Bud and to pass the information along to him in time.

In all this spying, Myra Maybelle was doing no more than many other young sisters and wives of soldiers, both from the North and the South. But unlike them, after Myra Maybelle's death she became the subject of all kinds of fanciful tales spun from thin air to flesh out the history of *Belle Starr, The Bandit Queen.*

The first such story, which may have had some basis in fact, was written by Samuel. W. Harman, who included it in his book, *Hell on the Border*, written in 1898. His story is full of misspellings and inaccurate dates, but in general it rings true.

Harman writes that on Myra Maybelle's sixteenth birthday she was returning from a scouting mission that had taken her eighteen miles from home. As she neared the small village of Newtonia she was surprised to find it occupied by Union forces. While there, she learned that a cavalry unit had already been dispatched to capture Bud Shirley, who was then visiting his family in Carthage.

Myra Maybelle was about to dash off to warn her brother when she was stopped by several Union troopers who prudently insisted she first meet their major. To Myra's dismay, she found herself face-to-face with a Major Eno, who had formerly lived in Carthage and had known Myra Maybelle and Bud as children. He recognized the girl immediately. No way was he going to let her loose now. Instead, he escorted her to the music room of the manor in which he had made his headquarters. He locked the door behind them and stood guard himself.

Myra burst into frantic tears. In her frustration, she began stamping around the room demanding to be let out. The major only laughed indulgently, amused by her antics. Now and then she would plump herself down on the piano stool and pound out a few measures of a popular song. Then she would resume her pacing, first pleading and then scolding shrilly, then back to the piano again to break the major's eardrums with her pounding on the keyboard.

Finally, believing his cavalry had had plenty of time to reach Carthage, the major unlocked the door and flung it open. Out flew Myra down the steps and to her horse, that still stood where she had left it. As she ran, she broke off several whips from the cherry bushes she passed. Once on her horse, she urged it to a gallop with stinging flicks of the cherry whip bundle.

The astonished major watched her streak across the stretch of open country and enter the tangled undergrowth of the woodlands beyond. Ignoring the beaten trail, Myra was taking a shortcut known only to her.

According to the story, Major Eno exclaimed, "If she doesn't reach Carthage ahead of my troopers, I'm a fool!"

The story ends with a description of Myra grooming her horse when the cavalry unit appeared. She greeted them with a curtsey and told them demurely that if they had come to see Bud Shirley, unfortunately he had left just half an hour ago.

Later writers, relying on their imagination, painted flashier backgrounds for the "Bandit Queen." One described her as a fierce warrior who had her own band of guerrillas. She had saved Bud that day by storming the house in which he was held captive and rescuing him. But no historical record supports this tale. Another story described Myra Maybelle as a member of Quantrill's band, riding with the James and Younger brothers on many daring raids. Handling a heavy pistol as adroitly as any of the others, she had killed four people by the time she was eighteen. This story, too, is contradicted by historical records that list the names of Quantrill's followers. The list contains the names of only two women, and neither one is Myra Maybelle.

Meanwhile, the war was grinding on. At the beginning, Southern spirits were high, for it looked as though the South were on the road to a quick victory. First, there had been the surrender of Fort Sumter to Rebel forces. This had been followed by the devastating defeat of Union forces at the Battle of Bull Run. That battle had left the road to Washington, D.C. wide open. If the

Southern army had followed through after its victory, the Union capital would have been an easy prize. But the South, too, had lost many men and was slow to follow its advantage, giving the Union forces time to recoup.

The South was not to have that advantage again. By 1863, the war was turning in favor of the North. In July of that year, the important Southern port of Vicksburg on the Mississippi River surrendered to Union forces. And in the same month, General Robert E. Lee's 78,000-man army was defeated at Gettysburg, though with great loss on both sides.

Yet the war continued as fiercely as ever. The whole state of Missouri was ravaged by roaming forces from both sides. Even the native tribes once banished to reserves were free to pillage from the hated white settlers wherever opportunities arose, indifferent to which side they were attacking.

In Jasper County, Union forces were still being bedeviled by Captain Bud Shirley and his band of guerrillas, now swollen to some forty members. They had become so dangerous to Union troops that they now had orders to shoot Bud Shirley on sight. But he continued to escape their traps until one fateful day late in June of 1864.

It happened in the village of Sarcoxie. At the time, Bud and a companion were enjoying a leisurely meal in the home of a Miss Stewart, a Southern sympathizer. Glancing out of a window, Bud and his friend caught sight of several Union soldiers stealing toward the house. They leapt from their unfinished meal and fled, racing across the field that stretched from the house to a fence. Both men reached the fence and leaped over it as gunfire rang out. Shirley received a direct hit as he made the leap and fell dead on the other side. His companion, only slightly injured, managed to escape on foot.

Miss Stewart's neighbor, Mrs. Sarah Musgrave, also a Southern sympathizer, rushed over to help her friend. Too late to do anything for Bud Shirley, they brought his body back to the Stewart home, where they began preparing it for delivery to Bud's father. Meanwhile, a messenger was sent to Carthage to inform the Shirley family of Bud's death.

According to Mrs. Musgrave's account, given in later years, ". . . [the] next day Shirley's mother and Myra Maybelle appeared in Sarcoxie, the latter with a belt around her waist from which hung two big revolvers on each side. She was not timid in making it known that she meant to get revenge for her brother's death . . ."

Other old timers recalled a somewhat different version of Bud's end. According to them, it was John Shirley, not his wife, who came with Myra Maybelle to retrieve Bud's corpse. While Myra waited in the wagon, her father entered the Stewart house to bring out his son's body. A group of Union troopers gathered as Myra watched her father lay the body of her brother in the back of the wagon and then go to the shed to unhitch Bud's horse. As he led the horse out and began tying him to the tailgate of the wagon, Miss Stewart brought out Bud's cap and belt with his gun holster attached to it and laid them on the seat beside Myra.

Myra stared at the belt and holster. Quickly she drew out the gun and fired it at the troopers. Her father rushed to stop her, but the troopers laughed derisively at every *click, click, click* of the gun. Finally Myra realized the men had already removed the bullets. Clutching the useless gun, she broke into sobs.

Her father, tight-lipped and grim, drove the team of horses down the trail to Carthage, so empty to him now that his beloved son on whom he had pinned so many hopes and dreams was dead. There was nothing left for him there. He stopped only long enough to bury his son and sell his properties at a great loss. Then he piled the family belongings into two wagons. With a subdued and heartbroken Myra driving one and he the other, the small caravan set out for Texas, where John Shirley's oldest son, Preston, had moved with his wife and children.

It was as well that they left when they did. Shortly after their departure, Northern troops and Southern guerrillas clashed again and again over Carthage. Finally a Southern band 200 strong stormed into the town and burned it to the ground, turning the once proud buildings into rubble. Scarcely a brick wall was left standing. Never again would Carthage offer hideaway or sanctuary to the hated Yankees.

Chapter Three

LIFE IN TEXAS

The Shirley wagons rolled out of the city of Carthage, traveling southward down the rutted trail, dust billowing from under the clattering hooves of the oxen and horses. The countryside that stretched away on both sides was a melancholy expanse of trampled fields, burnt ruins of little farmhouses, and low mounds of hastily dug graves, most without markers.

There were other travelers besides the Shirleys on the road. Disillusioned and crushed, the people of Missouri were heading south, with one goal in mind—the beautiful and free land of Canaan, as Texas was called.

For some years, others besides Missourians had been flocking to Texas. Among them were farmers from both the North and the South looking for better lands on the new frontier. Would-be ranchers came too, as well as thieves, cattle rustlers, confidence men, and escaped criminals. So many fugitives from justice were fleeing to Texas, where the laws were lax, that sheriffs in the eastern states often returned their warrants with the cryptic note GTT, *Gone to Texas.*

The Shirleys rolled toward this land of boundless opportunities and equally rampant lawlessness. From the lowlands, the wagons mounted the rocky tree-clad hills of the Ozark plateau. There, leaving Missouri behind, they crossed the border into Arkansas, continuing south until they came to Fort Smith on the Arkansas River. From Fort Smith they had several routes open to reach Preston Shirley's farm outside the little town of Scyene, a few miles south of Dallas. They crossed the Arkansas River by ferry, probably traveling south through Indian Territory. Presently, the Shirley wagons left the Ozark plateau behind and entered the wide sweep of prairie lands.

Toward the end of their journey, the Shirleys clattered down the muddy main street of Dallas. The town had been newly born out of the mud and dirt that year of 1864 to serve as a relay station for cattle drivers. Along the main street, shanties and tents were interspersed with rickety brothels, saloons, and gambling halls. The street swarmed with scruffy-looking men. There were cowpokes, tired from a long, grueling cattle drive, as well as well-dressed, slick-looking confidence men whose neat outfits stood out among the homespun clothing of the frontier folk. Thieves and outlaws were there in numbers, many drunk and brawling. To Myra, the rowdy settlement must have seemed a sharp contrast to the well-manicured town of Carthage.

It did not take long for the Shirleys to leave Dallas behind and plunge again into open prairie lands. Presently, they reached Scyene and drew up in front of Preston's home. While Preston discussed conditions in Texas with his father, Myra and her two brothers made the acquaintance of Preston's children. John Shirley planned to return to his life as a farmer. It did not take him long to pick the area he wanted for himself. His expert eye recognized the fine black, fertile soil, ideal for raising crops. Once he had ownership of it, Shirley created living quarters for his family by digging a large hole in the side of a nearby hill. He shaped it into a large room. The family would live in this dugout until a real house could be built. Such dugouts were common on prairie lands, where wood was scarce.

With the family settled, Shirley put his new holdings under the plow. Other farmers in the area were cultivating cotton. The rich soil and favorable climate promised good yields. But John chose to plant the crops that had given him so much success in Missouri—corn and sorghum. On the side, he planned to raise hogs and horses for sale.

The Shirleys earned the ill will of the neighbors the first days on their farm. Old timers there had learned to share the communal well water, drawing out only what they needed, since the well took a long time to refill. At first, the Shirleys thoughtlessly drained the well by filling a huge water barrel to the brim to save themselves from making frequent trips to get water. It took them a while to repair relationships with their indignant neighbors.

Once farming was underway John Shirley provided a proper house for his family. He hauled in enough expensive logs to build a solid four-room log cabin. Back in Missouri, it would have looked like any other small farmhouse, but in the almost treeless Texas prairie, their cabin was considered a mansion.

Still intent on keeping up their daughter's education, the Shirleys sent Myra to the local school. Myra attended the one-room school that served all the children in the area, but soon found it boring. Back in Carthage, she had already covered all the subjects they were teaching here. Most of the students were younger, and she found nothing in common with those few who were her own age. How could she have? She once had been known as the richest girl in Carthage, admired by everyone for her daring spy work during the Civil War. Here she was just another displaced person, scarcely noticed by her classmates.

Myra came to hate school so much that she started skipping classes to help around the house. Her favorite chore was hoeing up weeds in the family garden. When Myra wanted company, she visited Preston's children in Scyene. But she enjoyed most the long lonely horseback rides she took. Myra's rides usually ended at the little town of Mesquite Creek. There she would make query after query about news coming from Missouri, especially from Carthage. She was desperately homesick for some contact with the life she had left behind.

✳ Belle Starr

One day she returned from her ride to find exciting
visitors at the Shirley home: the famous Younger brothers
and Frank and Jesse James. During the war years, Cole
Younger had been a frequent visitor at the Shirley home
in Carthage.

After the war, which ended in April of 1865, the
Younger and James boys felt dispossessed and bitter over
their treatment by Northern officers who now had full
control of Missouri. They responded by becoming outlaws. In the weeks and months that followed General
Lee's surrender of his Southern army at Appomatox, they
continued their brand of guerrilla warfare by committing
a string of daring bank, train, and stagecoach robberies,
always escaping one step ahead of the sheriffs and their
posses. Most of their success was due to the efforts of
Southern admirers who still honored them as heroes and
were eager to protect them in any way they could.

Myra's father welcomed his guests warmly. After a
hearty meal prepared by Eliza, the visitors regaled the
family with stories of their recent adventures. They also
brought news of friends the Shirleys had left behind. The
excitement young Myra felt at their coming lingered for
many days.

In later years, some biographers of Belle Starr were to
write that during Cole's visits to the Shirley home, he and
Myra had a wild love affair, resulting in an illegitimate
child. In the autobiography he wrote years later, Cole
denied the story. Myra, while admitting that she had given

her heart to a dashing guerrilla, said it was not Cole, but a young man named Jim Reed.

Myra had first met Jim when she was thirteen years old, and he was almost fifteen. That was back in 1861, when Kansas Jayhawkers were attacking farms in the vicinity of Rich Hill, where the Reeds had a farm. Afraid for the safety of their ten children, the Reeds moved temporarily to Carthage. It was there that Myra met Jim, the Reeds' fourth son. Unlike his more adventurous brothers, he was then a gentle, religious boy, always ready to help his mother in any way he could.

Jim's father, Solomon Reed, and John Shirley had become good friends, and Jim and Myra had begun seeing a great deal of each other at school. But their growing attachment was cut short when things became safer around Rich Hill, and the Reed family returned to their neglected farm. By the time Jim, a skinny sharp-featured teenager, had reached his seventeenth birthday, the frenzy of war had caught him up, and he joined Quantrill.

With Lee's surrender, Quantrill's guerrilla bands broke up. The Reed boys came home, but to a saddened family. That year, their father died suddenly of a heart attack, and their mother decided to visit relatives in Texas in search of comfort. She left, taking her younger children, including Jim, with her.

The Reed relatives lived in Scyene, not far from the Shirley home, and Jim was able to resume his interrupted romance with Myra. Later writers were to paint a fanciful tale of how the couple, fleeing from the wrath of both their families, eloped and were married on horseback by a justice of the peace.

Actually, the wedding was quite normal. Myra was eighteen and Jim twenty when he proposed to her and she accepted. Jim procured the necessary marriage license, and the wedding was held in a little church in Collin County by the Reverend S. M. Wilkins on November 1, 1866.

After the wedding, Jim stayed with the Shirley family and helped with the work. But after his exciting escapades with Quantrill's guerrillas, the day-by-day routines of farm life bored him. In 1867, he took a job in Dallas selling saddles and bridles. He often spoke of getting some land for himself and raising horses and cattle. John Shirley offered to help his son-in-law locate some suitable acreage but never got around to it. When Jim's mother decided to return to the family farm near Rich Hill, Jim and Myra went with her.

There, in early September 1868, Myra gave birth to a daughter whom she named Rosie Lee. At the first glimpse of her little blonde baby, Myra's heart turned over with love and pride. From that moment on, Myra always called Rosie Lee "Pearl," the most precious gem in her life.

The birth of the child was followed by news of the violent death of Myra's brother Edwin. The circumstances that caused it were described in one brief sentence in a Dallas newspaper: "Ed Shirley, a noted horse thief, was shot off his horse near Dallas in 1868."

Myra, who had always been devoted to her brothers, probably returned to Scyene briefly for Edwin's funeral and to show off little Pearl to her grandparents. After the funeral Myra did not stay long in Texas, eager as she was to return to her new life and her husband in Missouri.

Chapter Four

THE FUGITIVES

Myra enjoyed the first year of married life at Rich Hill. She was close enough to Carthage now to renew old friendships and display her little daughter, Pearl. Compared to her lively and often rambunctious behavior during the war years, Myra now behaved demurely. Old-time parishioners of Rich Hill's Bethel Baptist Church remembered long afterward how Myra went to church every Sunday. Riding sidesaddle on her horse and carrying Pearl dressed in Sunday finery, she would arrive, tether her horse, go into the church and seat herself in a front pew. Throughout the pastor's long, wordy sermon, Myra would sit primly, never once even glancing at him but fixing her rapt gaze on her sleeping baby.

Jim seemed as proud of the little girl as Myra. But as the months wore on, Myra began to see less and less of him. Like some of his brothers, he still craved the excitement of his Quantrill days and began to spend his time in Fort Smith, where he and his brothers joined a gang run by a man named John K. Fisher. The gang spent a lot of time cattle rustling in Indian Territory. Whatever money they got, they squandered in Fort Smith saloons or gambling halls, where fortunes were lost or won on a single throw of the dice.

Eventually, the Fisher gang got into a heated quarrel over a gambling debt with another gang run by the Shannon brothers. As the quarrel spun out of control, two members of the Shannon gang shot Scott Reed as he crossed a street. The Shannons promptly pleaded they had shot the wrong man by mistake and expressed their remorse for the killing. But Jim still was unsatisfied. Southern honor demanded that he avenge Scott's death. He tracked down the two killers and shot them on the spot.

After the shooting, Jim raced home and told Myra what had happened, ordering her to pack at once. They had to leave town quickly, he explained, and go as far away as they could before the Shannons came to take their revenge on the whole family. California was his destination.

Myra did not argue, certainly not when the life of her baby was threatened. She packed, took Pearl, and went to the nearest stagecoach station, probably Atchison, where she boarded a coach heading west. By this time, Jim had left on horseback, going by out-of-the-way routes to keep from being recognized.

For close to three weeks, Myra and little Pearl traveled the long route that was still the shortest way to California.

They rolled and bounced along through corn fields that gave way to wide prairies and into a land growing more and more barren as it mounted upward into the Rocky Mountains. Myra had never seen these towering mountains. On the far side, the coach rolled down into a land of jumbled red rock, carved by water and wind into fantastic shapes. Beyond the jumble, the travelers entered the valley of the Great Salt Lake, settled by Mormons. They left Salt Lake City behind and continued on down the valley and then up through the passes in the mountains that hemmed the western boundary of the valley. And there beyond, as far as the eye could see, shimmered the dry, waterless deserts of central Nevada.

Day after day after day, Myra sat squeezed between two other passengers while the coach swayed and bounced. Her shoulders were bruised and her neck and back ached. Most nights, she had to sleep on the moving coach until the ride became a throbbing, aching montage to her. As the miles rolled away, Myra wondered what life would be like so far from friends and family in this increasingly strange and threatening land. As she worried, she clutched her little daughter closer to her.

Finally, they ascended the last barrier range—the pinnacled Sierra Nevadas, their sharp peaks leaping into the sky. Up, up along narrow trails that twisted and turned, the coach bounced. Then down again, down into a wide valley of vineyards, ranches, and wheat fields. Suddenly Myra's spirits rose. It seemed like such a kind and friendly land. The mountains that had formerly appeared to be stern barriers standing between her and every familiar thing she knew now became a protective shield standing between her and the past. Here, she and Jimmie, as she called him, could settle down and begin life anew.

At Sacramento, Myra took the stagecoach south to Los Angeles, traveling through the same platter of well-tended countryside. Finally they reached the bustling town, where Jim was waiting for them. In the days ahead, Myra and Jim planned their future. Farming was the answer for Myra, and Jim went along with the idea.

The couple left Los Angeles for the little village of Los Nietos standing on the San Gabriel River not far from the city. The tiny village was surrounded by thriving farm-lands. Though only a modest amount of rain fell here, the river provided plenty of water for irrigation. It was a good place to settle down. Jim and Myra made a down payment on forty-seven acres of land, borrowing money to do so.

On February 22, 1871, shortly after settling in Los Nietos, Myra gave birth to her second child, a boy whom they called James Edwin—James after his father, and Edwin to honor Myra's recently slain brother. The child soon was nicknamed Eddie. To earn money until they could make a profit from their farm, Jim began taking odd jobs in Los Angeles. He bartended in the saloons that lined the main business streets of the city. He filled in as a croupier in some of the numerous gambling halls. With the nest egg they had brought from Rich Hill, the couple was able to stay afloat for a while. But one dark cloud still marred their happiness. It was the due date of the $400 loan. They would never be able to pay it unless they had help from someone. Finally, Jim got Myra to write a letter to his brother Marion, who was one of the more stable members of the Reed family.

"We will make a permanent home here," Myra wrote in her very long letter which was dated California, 1872. "I think in a few years we can have as lovely a place as this state can boast of . . ." She goes on to describe their plans in glowing terms—fields of grain, vegetable gardens, eventually even a vineyard.

Finally Myra got to the problem she and Jim faced, their shortage of cash. She begged Marion to come out west and share their venture with them. If he could not do that, would he at least lend them the necessary money to pay off their debt?

Marion refused to come to California or lend the money. As if this were not bad enough, Jim suddenly found himself in serious trouble with the law. He was accused of passing counterfeit currency in the gambling halls where he was acting as croupier. Since this was a federal crime, federal agents immediately began investigating Jim. They could not find any real proof that he had knowingly passed the counterfeit bills. But they did discover something much worse—James Reed was currently wanted for murder in the state of Arkansas. Armed with a warrant, the agents were preparing to arrest Jim when he heard of it. So, in late March of 1872, a little less than two years after the family had come west in the hope of making a new life for themselves, they were on the run again. And they had to move fast to keep ahead of the law.

Once more Myra packed up their belongings. Before leaving, she dressed three-year-old Pearl in boys' clothes in case federal agents posted spies at every stop to arrest her and the children with the hope of forcing Jim to surrender. Since they would be looking for a young mother with a year-old boy and a little girl, they might overlook a mother with two little boys.

Jim had already left by the time Myra and the two children boarded the stagecoach in Los Angeles and started on the long return journey. While the coach bounced and rattled over rutty trails, up and down mountains, and across deserts, Myra considered her bleak future. So far, her life had consisted of running from place to place, and the children, tired and whimpering, now had to suffer this disjointed gypsy life as well. She asked herself if it were worth it.

By the time they crossed the Rockies, Myra's mind was made up. She refused to run any more, nor would she return to the Reed farm in Missouri. Instead she would join her parents in Texas, where she planned to stay.

Myra and the children found eager arms awaiting them in Scyene. Eliza, especially, had been missing her daughter and the two little grandchildren. She had been pleading with her husband to take the risk with what he must have regarded as an unworthy son-in-law and deed over part of his extensive holdings to the young couple. During one of his visits to the Shirley home, Cole Younger had backed Eliza's idea. At last, John Shirley agreed and signed over a large parcel of land to Jim and Myra. Eliza cut some of the calves and cows out of her own herd to launch the new farm. There must have been some kind of small house on the property, perhaps built by John Shirley or his son-in-law for Myra and the children.

Jim Reed joined Myra in Texas, enthusiastic to begin their new venture. He pitched in with zeal, not only working the new farm but helping out the neighbors as well. They found him to be a pleasant young man, always ready to assist in any way he could. Myra was accepted also, a young mother raising two very small children.

When a rash of cattle rustling broke out in the vicinity, Jim's neighbors were impressed with his fervent pledge to help them capture or drive out the thieves. But as cattle began to disappear one by one from the farms and small ranches that were in the area surrounding the Reed home, the neighbors became suspicious, especially when they realized that the thefts had started only after the Reeds arrived. Just as unsettling were the shifty-eyed visitors who kept showing up at the Reed home.

As suspicions hardened to certainty, the angry neighbors turned on the Reeds. If it weren't for the good name Myra's parents enjoyed in the area, Jim would probably have been reported at once to the local sheriff. Instead, he was warned that unless the thieving stopped, the law would be called in.

Jim made no admission of guilt, but after the warning, his shady friends stopped visiting the Reed home. Jim also began staying away, just as he had at Rich Hill. Drifting from gang to gang, he began committing a series of crimes: thefts of valuable race horses, cows, burglaries of homes and small shops. These crimes provided him with the cash he needed for his heavy drinking and gambling sprees.

Now and then, Jim came home to visit his family and to work around the farm. But that quickly bored him, and despite Myra's reproaches about the kind of life he was leading, Jim would eventually slip away from home as stealthily as he had come.

Chapter Five

AN OUTLAW DIES

Jim Reed continued to drift from gang to gang, carrying his activities farther and farther afield until the sheriffs of several counties were out looking for him. Whenever the chase got too close, Jim would go to hiding places provided by various friends. He did not dare go home again. Instead, he would send Myra a message asking her to meet him. Myra would leave the children with her parents and join him until the hunt for him cooled. Then Jim, despite Myra's protests, would go back to his old way of life and Myra would return home.

Finally on February 17, 1873, Jim stepped over the line. Four men heard that a local businessman named Dick Cravey had a large stash of money hidden in his home. One evening the four went to Cravey's door and knocked. When he opened the door, a blast from four guns mowed him down. His attackers rushed over his body to ransack the house in search of the cash. They found only a modest amount of money.

An uproar followed the killing. There were dark suspicions that the Reed brothers, Jim and Sol, who had recently moved to Texas, were two of the killers, but there was no proof against them. Then on August 7, Jim and Sol struck openly. Execution style, they killed a man named Wheeler, once their trusted friend. Not only was Wheeler killed, but his tongue was cut out too—a warning to all would-be informers. This time there was no doubt about the brothers' guilt, and warrants were issued for their arrest, backed by a $500 bounty on each of them.

Sol had had enough. He fled to Missouri and the warrant against him had to be dropped. Jim chose to scoff at the warrant and the money on his head. More determined than ever to get a lucky strike that would make him rich, he committed his most daring robbery. On November 19, 1873, he and two other men, all masked, entered the Indian Territory and kidnapped Judge Grayson, a wealthy Creek and former Supreme Court justice now retired. Rumor claimed he had a large amount of money hidden somewhere on his premises.

The three men tried threats to force Judge Grayson to tell them where the treasure was. When that did not work, they dropped a noose around his neck and threw the rope over a tree limb. They began pulling him up and down, up and down, half strangling him each time. But even when he was close to death, Judge Grayson refused to talk. The men strung up his wife and started hanging her as they had done to the Judge. After watching his wife nearly choked to death three times, the judge gave up and showed the men where the money was buried under his house.

According to Judge Grayson the robbers left with some $30,000 in coins and gold bullion—his life savings—which they divided among themselves. Jim squandered his share drinking and gambling while planning a new crime with his three friends.

It took a while for the law to identify the assailants. Their identification rested on the testimony of Judge Grayson, who described them as large white men. More importantly, the judge was able to describe one of the horses—a bay mare, her sides freckled with spots and what looked like a white star on her forehead. The uniquely marked horse was easily recognized as belonging to a close friend of Jim Reed.

With Jim now named as a kidnapper, Myra became a target for rumors that spread throughout Texas and the Indian Territory. Some stories said that she was one of the three bandits disguised as a man. Judge Grayson shot that idea down. It was impossible, he said, because Myra was a petite woman and his assailants were big, burly men. But the rumors which did not stop were built on Myra's colorful life as a Civil War spy and now the wife of a brutal outlaw.

As for Jim, he was finding himself in even greater danger because of the $1,500 bounty now on his head. He became increasingly uneasy about trusting the friends who had been hiding him. There was only one man on whose loyalty he felt he could depend. His name was Tom Starr, a Cherokee chief.

The Cherokee people, along with the Choctaw, Chickasaw, Creek, and Senecas, were not indigenous to this area. Their original home had been in the eastern states of Georgia, the Carolinas, Tennessee, Alabama, and Mississippi. The tribes already led settled lives as prosperous farmers. After the white settlers moved in, they learned the ways of the newcomers and opened schools, developed a written language, and adopted the legal system. Because of their adoption of these white ways, they became known as the Five Civilized Tribes.

At first, the Five Civilized Tribes were accepted as equals by their white neighbors. But as more and more white people came to the area, clashes broke out between them and the tribespeople. To relieve the growing tension, the United States offered the tribes the newly acquired territory which was later to become the state of Oklahoma. They were told they could establish their own nations there and live according to their own tribal laws and regulations without interference.

Around 1818, the first group of tribes traveled west to take advantage of this offer. In 1835, gold was found in Georgia and the Carolinas and a stampede of would-be prospectors swarmed into those states. Crowded out of their homeland, a second wave of eastern tribes started making the long journey westward.

Finally in August of 1838, the third and largest wave of tribespeople was forced out by soldiers. Pushed and hurried along, 15,000 Native Americans began the difficult trek westward. Men, women and children, the old and the very young, struggled on foot, poorly clothed, suffering heat and cold, half starved on scanty rations. Some drowned in fast-running rivers. Others died of starvation and diseases—dysentery, measles, mumps, and pneumonia. Out of the 15,000 who set out, at least 4,000 died along the way. The terrible journey came to be known as the Trail of Tears.

Once the newcomers reached Oklahoma, war broke out between them and the earlier arrivals. Oklahoma became a bloody battlefield. The struggle went on for years. But by the Civil War, the various factions had finally made peace with one another. Each of the Five Civilized Tribes established its own nation where its people lived by their own laws.

During the tribal wars, Tom Starr's father, James Starr, had been a feared warrior until assassins took his life. His son Tom had followed in his father's footsteps. Now fifty-five years of age, Tom Starr was an imposing figure, standing six feet five inches tall, broad shouldered, and muscular. His long thick hair had turned white. Beneath the thatch of bushy eyebrows, gray eyes as cold as steel revealed the presence of some white blood in his parentage. Tom Starr was known as a loyal friend and a ruthless enemy. He wore the proof of that around his neck, a necklace strung of the withered earlobes of the enemies he had slain.

Starr had sided with the Southern cause. He had been a close ally and friend of Quantrill and the Youngers, who had visited him frequently. It was even said that he had passed along Cherokee war strategies to Quantrill. Whenever any of the guerrillas were in danger of capture, they would retreat south to find sanctuary with Starr.

After the war ended, the Youngers continued to visit the powerful chief from time to time. If they were ever in trouble with the law, they knew they could find protection with him. So it was natural for Jim to turn to old Tom for sanctuary now. The chief welcomed him warmly, and Reed began staying with him every time the pressure from eager sheriffs and their posses became too great. From Tom Starr's sanctuary, Jim would send a note to Myra asking her to join him. Then Myra would leave her children and come at once, traveling by secret ways into Indian Territory where the white sheriffs could not follow without being invited.

Myra was always to remember these times, when she felt closer to her husband than she had for a long while. The couple would go on spirited horseback rides through the territory, and if a dance was being held in the area they would set off for it, even though it might be twenty or thirty miles away. The dances were social events usually put on by the few white women married to tribal people living in the area.

Dressed in their best and accompanied by Tom Starr's teenage son Sam, who acted as a bodyguard, they would set off for a night of merriment that might last well into the next day. Though liquor was forbidden in Indian Territory, it flowed abundantly at these parties. If the hostess had a piano, she would join the fiddler and perhaps a guitarist to beat out the notes of some popular tune. Then the guests catching the beat would whirl and glide and stamp the night away. Dancing in Jim's arms, Myra could forget the dark underworld of her husband's life, where victims lay dead and sheriffs waited in ambush.

One day, Myra received an alarming message from Jim. There were rumors she was being shadowed to discover the secret route she used to slip into Indian Territory to visit him. If the lawmen could discover that route, they would set a trap for Jim. Myra was instructed to stay at Starr's place permanently. So Myra left her children with her parents and set off again for the Starr home. There she waited for her husband—day after day, week after week, wondering, worrying. What had gone wrong? Had they caught him? Was he shot down?

Finally the news arrived, passed along on the human grapevine: Jim Reed was not coming because he was having a torrid love affair with a beautiful eighteen-year-old Mexican girl named Rosa. He had even promised to marry her.

Myra was in a turmoil of hurt and anger. At age twenty-six, she was still attractive, but no match against beautiful Rosa. All the years of loyalty she had given her husband, even to the ruin of her own reputation, had only brought her this betrayal. Myra was finished with Jim. She left the Starr home and hurried back to her family.

Jim knew nothing of what was happening with Myra. Holed up in a hotel in San Antonio with Rosa and three of his male friends, he had embarked on a long spree of drinking while planning the next venture—this time a bold stagecoach holdup. The plan in place, Jim told Rosa bluntly that he had never intended to marry her, and he deserted her in San Antonio, penniless and far from her family. Then, he and his friends set off to carry out the holdup.

On April 7, 1874, the stagecoach heading for Austin, Texas, was within twenty-three miles of the city when in the lengthening afternoon it was brought to a sudden halt by three gunmen. They cut loose the lead horses and chased them away. Then they ordered the driver and nine passengers, one of whom was a woman, out of the coach. They searched them at gunpoint, stripping them of any watches or jewelry. Afterward they went to the coach, broke the locks on the passengers' trunks and searched through them for valuable objects. Finally they opened the United States mail bags and sorted through letters and packages for currency or cashable money orders. At last they were done. They filled one of the bags with their loot, turned the remaining horses loose, and drove them away too. Then, putting spurs to their own horses, they rode off, leaving behind the terrified passengers shivering in the deepening twilight.

The driver calmed his charges, then walked to the next station some three miles away to get fresh horses. He brought them back, harnessed them to the coach and urged the passengers to gather up their scattered belongings while he took care of the mail. Finally everyone boarded and they were off again, arriving in Austin at daybreak.

News of the holdup had traveled ahead of them and reporters were already at the stagecoach station waiting to question the passengers. They praised the driver as a hero and expressed regret at the loss of their property. But they also voiced their gratitude for the professional manner in which the outlaws had acted. No one had been injured and no lives lost.

The state legislature acted quickly. It passed a bill offering a $3,000 reward for the apprehension of the bandits. The agent for the United States mail added another $3,000 to the reward, and the manager of the stagecoach line offered $1,000.

With a $7,000 reward being offered, Texas and the Indian Territory soon began crawling with would-be bounty hunters. It took all the wiles of the fugitives, along with the help of their secret friends, to evade their pursuers. The fugitives soon realized how dangerous it was for them to be traveling together. They split up, each going his separate way. During Jim's flight, he was accompanied by a new friend, John T. Morris, whom he met shortly after the holdup. For three months, Morris stuck close to Jim, proving his loyalty by apparently taking many risks to protect him from discovery. Jim came to trust him completely. What Jim did not know was that Morris had been secretly deputized to bring him in, dead or alive.

On the eve of the sixth of August, as Jim and Morris were approaching Indian Territory, Morris realized he would lose his chance to get Jim if he escaped across the border. He suggested they stop at a mutual friend's house near the town of Paris, Texas, to spend the night.

Jim agreed and they entered the home. While Jim was sitting at the dining table, Morris saw his chance. He pulled his gun out and leveled it at Jim, ordering him to surrender. Instead Jim slipped under the table and rose holding the table top like a shield between him and Morris. He began retreating to the door, cursing himself for letting Morris talk him into leaving his gun outside with the horses.

Morris fired three times. The last bullet pierced the table top and Reed dropped dead, shot through the heart. Morris, his eyes glinting at the thought of the bounty, which had now risen to $7,500, took Jim's corpse to Paris.

A popular story tells how Morris immediately contacted Myra and asked her to come and identify the corpse. He was sure she would because of the way Jim had betrayed her. Myra answered the summons promptly. Astride her favorite horse, she rode to the place where the corpse lay. She took one scornful look at it and declared loudly and firmly, "I never saw him in my life before." Then turning to stare at Morris she added, "You will never get that bounty." And whirling on her heel, she mounted her horse and rode off. It was her last gift of loyalty and love for her faithless husband.

It is a nice story, but in truth Myra's testimony was unnecessary. There were plenty of others who knew Jim Reed well and could identify his body. As for Morris, he benefited little from his treachery. He had brought in only one of the four criminals the authorities had identified as the holdup men. His share was one-fourth of the $7,500 bounty—a mere $1,700, for which he had risked his life for three long months.

Chapter Six

WANDERING, WANDERING

After her husband's death, Myra would have been almost penniless, except for the farm her father had deeded to her. She worried most about her daughter's future. In those days, it was almost impossible for a woman to support herself independently of a man. Myra had noticed how popular little-girl performers were in frontier towns. One of these children, pretty Lotta Crabtree, had made a name for herself in California gold towns and had grown up to do world tours. She had become an international star. Why not Pearl?

When Myra broached the idea to her parents, they were shocked and spoke vehemently against the idea. It was an unfit occupation for a lady. But Myra was determined. Leaving Eddie with her mother, she set off for Dallas with Pearl and enrolled the child in a public school and also in an acting class.

Dallas must have dazzled Pearl, fresh from the quiet village of Scyene. The muddy little town her mother had first seen was now transformed into a bustling city, its tents and shanties giving way to imposing brick buildings.

The city had become a rail center. Rails fanned out north, south, and west. Cattle were the big shipping commodity. Most of the shipments went south to the port of Galveston, where they would be carried by ship to the east coast.

Though Dallas had become a major Texas city, it still retained much of its raucous spirit. It swarmed with cowpokes ready to whoop it up at the end of a long cattle drive. There were plenty of saloons, gambling halls, and brothels to suit their taste. Gamblers, thieves, and prostitutes swarmed to take the money of the unwary. There were also the usual wild souls indulging in shootouts without any danger of being locked up because police were too scarce.

Later biographies of Belle Starr liked to embellish their narratives with stories describing Myra's antics in Dallas, turning her into one of these unbridled characters. They pictured her sorties down Main Street, brandishing her six-shooters and firing them off at intervals, sending pedestrians scattering. They told how she swaggered into saloons, downing her whiskey in man-sized gulps; how she lured wealthy men into her net to fleece them; how she owned a livery stable stocked with stolen horses.

But these wild stories were written about Belle long after her death. The local newspapers at the time never once mentioned Myra's escapades, though they covered every activity in the city, from the pickpockets to the hardcore criminals. And they certainly embellished their columns with tales of colorful Dallas characters. It is Myra herself who provides the most accurate account of how she spent the first two years following Jim's death. In a long letter to her mother-in-law dated August 10, 1876, Myra begins:

"Dear Mother, Brothers and Sisters:

"I write you after so long a time to let you know that I am still alive. Time has made many changes and some very sad indeed . . ."

She goes on to tell how on July 10, her father, John Shirley, died, leaving a large gap in their lives. Then her eighteen-year-old brother Cravens, nicknamed Shug, had gotten into serious trouble with the law and had fled Texas. Her mother, Eliza, whose finances were not so good, was selling her farm and moving to Dallas with her grandson Eddie.

Of Eddie, Myra writes: "He is a fine manly looking boy as you ever seen and I don't think there is a more intelligent boy living. You would love him for the sake of the dear one's that's gone."

Myra continues with news of Pearl, using the child's given name: "Rosie is here in Dallas going to school. She has the reputation of being the prettiest little girl in Dallas. She is learning very fast. She had been playing here in the Dallas theatre and gained a worldwide reputation for her prize performance. My people were very much opposed to it but I wanted her to be able to make a living of her own, without depending on anyone . . ."

Then Myra complains about the disloyalty of her husband's brothers. She points out that when Scott Reed was killed, Jim avenged his death by shooting his assailants. Then why did Sol not come to avenge Jim's death at the hands of the faithless Morris? She adds sadly that if Sol had only done this she would have gladly given him Jim's favorite horse, Rondo, worth $200.

Myra finally gets to personal matters. The renters of the various parcels of land into which her farm was divided had not been tending them properly. "So I made nothing," Myra concludes. "I am going to sell this fall if I can." And she ends the letter with, "I am far from well. I am so nervous this evening from the headache that I can scarcely write."

Two or three months after Myra wrote this letter, another catastrophe struck, this time involving little Pearl. In the midst of a performance, she collapsed on stage and was rushed to the hospital. The doctor who examined her diagnosed the ailment as "a sudden rush of blood to the brain." Pearl hovered between life and death. Eventually she recovered, but her physician warned Myra that she should no longer push the child to perform for fear of relapse.

Myra's dream of Pearl's stage success burst like a bubble. But in its place came a new dream. She would groom Pearl to be a lady, the wife of a respectable and wealthy businessman who would provide her with every security. Meanwhile, Eddie was proving too much for Eliza, whose health was poor, so Myra sent him to grandmother Shirley where his aunts and uncles could help take care of him. Then with the proceeds from the sale of her farm, Myra took Pearl with her and set out on a leisurely journey visiting old Carthage friends and former schoolmates who were scattered throughout Missouri, Arkansas, and Kansas.

In Conway, Arkansas, Myra decided to leave Pearl with a longtime friend. After making sure that her daughter was happy there, Myra continued on her restless travels. In 1879, her journey took her to Joplin, Missouri, where another old friend lived. From Joplin, Myra took a side trip to the mining town of Galena, where she met a little-known member of the Younger family: Bruce Younger, cousin to Cole Younger. Though a wastrel, Myra found him exciting at first. The two struck up a friendship that ripened into much more. Myra moved to Galena, taking a room at the hotel where Bruce was staying.

Soon people began seeing Bruce and Myra together everywhere. Tongues started wagging when the couple began frequenting Redhot Street, Bruce's favorite hang-out. The street was lined with gambling joints, saloons, dance halls, and brothels. Bruce was well known there as a tinhorn gambler, and it was rumored that when he won big he would shower Myra with money and expensive gifts. People whispered that Myra and Bruce, though unmarried, were even sharing a hotel room.

The hotel owner contradicted this. He said he did not know about any marriage, but he could say with certainty that Myra had a room of her own. Her mother and brother Shug sometimes came to visit her there. And Pearl came along for visits too, a pretty little girl of eight or nine. The hotel owner's opinion of Myra Maybelle was that she was "a mighty good looking woman, well educated, quietly dressed, not tough like the newspapers said."

When Myra, tiring of Galena, decided to return to Indian Territory to visit Tom Starr, Bruce must have accompanied her. They were still not married, but Myra obviously expected that to happen, for she changed her daughter's name from Reed to Younger.

After staying a while in Indian Territory, Bruce Younger tired of the quiet life and of Myra as well. Instead of marrying her as she had expected, he quietly slipped out of town. From the Cherokee she learned that he was heading north for Kansas.

Younger had used her, Myra thought, had ruined her reputation by promising marriage, and now was throwing her away like a discarded bit of clothing. There is a saucy story describing how she got her revenge. It goes like this:

Myra, learning of Bruce's deceit, leapt astride her favorite horse and sped off for Kansas where she went to the nearby courthouse and procured a marriage license.

She rooted out a minister or justice of the peace and descended on the unwary Bruce, waving the license at him. Pointing her pistol at his head, she told him she would blow his brains out if he refused to marry her at once. In front of twenty witnesses, the cowed Bruce spoke his vows. The minister concluded the brief service with the time-honored words: "I now pronounce you man and wife." Myra ordered a keg of beer, told the cheering crowd to celebrate the occasion, and galloped back to Indian Territory alone.

This might be regarded as just another wild tale, except for the evidence of the marriage record in Labette County, Kansas. It states that Bruce Younger and Maybelle Reed were wed in Chetopa, Kansas. The date was May 15, 1880.

Chapter Seven

MYRA MARRIES AGAIN

Myra had not suffered a broken heart over Bruce Younger, whose shifty nature had begun to repulse her. She was already falling for Tom Starr's son Sam, who had so often acted as bodyguard during Jim's visits to Indian Territory. Sam was twenty-three years old by this time and no longer a gangly boy.

Three-quarters Cherokee and one-quarter white, he was slender and athletic. There was an alertness and grace about his every movement that caught the eye of those who met him. As one man put it, he had a face "like a picture." Astride his bay pony, cantering down the road, men as well as women admiringly turned to watch him.

Despite Sam's quarter-white blood, he was a true Cherokee, proud of his ancient past, treasuring his heritage. He wanted nothing to do with anything white civilization had to offer. He spoke only broken English and could not read or write that language because he had refused to attend the public schools.

Myra was drawn to Sam for his masculinity. Sam was overwhelmed by the force of Myra's personality. Some three weeks after Myra's marriage to Bruce Younger, she and Sam were married by Cherokee law. The following document appears in the court records of the Cherokee Nation:

> STARR & REED On the 5th day of June 1880 by Abe Woodall—District Judge for the Canadian Dist. C. N.—Samuel Starr a citizen of Cherokee Nation age 23 years and Mrs. Bell [sic] Reed a citizen of the United States age 27 years. H. J. Vann, Clerk

In the wedding license, Myra Maybelle lopped off five years from her true age. She also ignored the farcical wedding she had forced on Bruce Younger, using instead the surname of her first husband, Jim Reed. From the day she married Sam Starr she began using the name "Belle," taken from her middle name Maybelle, and would be known from then on simply as Belle Starr.

Tom Starr welcomed the new bride into his extended family. He lent the couple the use of a tiny house near his, while they looked for their own parcel of land. Cherokee law did not permit members to own land privately. But they could apply to receive any free parcel they wished to develop. This privilege was denied to whites unless they were married to a Cherokee who could make the claim.

Sam left the selection of the land to Belle. Wishing to cut herself off from her former friends and associates, she looked for a private place. She finally settled on the most isolated spot she could find. It bordered the north bank of the Canadian River at its great bend.

The steep cliffs that lined a long stretch of the river were pocked with caves. Legend said they had been the hiding places of Southern guerrillas fleeing from Union soldiers. Meadowlands stretched from the north bank of the river to tree-clad hills that dissolved into mountains. The place was known as Youngers' Bend because during Civil War days the Youngers had often come there to map out their future strategies.

The water in the river was too silty for use, but a bubbling spring fed a little creek that flowed nearby, providing fresh water for the household. Sam was as pleased as Belle with the selection of Youngers' Bend. Everything they would need was at hand. There was even a livable cabin standing on a rock-strewn rise of land. It provided a good view across the meadows to the mouth of the narrow canyon, the only entrance to Youngers' Bend. From the cabin, an intruder could be easily spotted before he cleared the canyon mouth. Behind the cabin, thick woodlands formed a dark green shelter in which fugitives could find instant cover.

Belle chose Youngers' Bend as the site of her new home with Sam Starr. *(Photograph by Fred S. Barde, Fred S. Barde College. Courtesy of the Archives & Manuscripts Division of the Oklahoma Historical Society, 1464.4.)*

Built of cedar logs, the cabin had a shingle roof. It had only one room, fourteen feet square. A rafted ceiling rose some seven feet above the neatly tooled log floor. There was one small window. A lean-to at the rear of the cabin was divided into two small rooms. A cellar dug beneath the rooms made a good storage space for perishable goods on hot days.

The cabin had formerly been the home of an old Cherokee named Big Head, who was now dead. He was rumored to have amassed a treasure of gold that he had buried somewhere nearby. Some people claimed that Belle and Sam spent their spare time digging up the ground around the cabin searching for that treasure. Whether Belle searched for treasure or not, she spent a lot of her spare time fixing up the cabin for the guest she hoped would soon be joining them there—her daughter Pearl.

The Cherokee traditionally used gaudy muslin to cover the walls of their cabins. Belle chose white calico decorated with dainty flower designs. She bought the necessary furniture, which included beds, a table, chairs, cooking utensils, and a kerosene lamp. She decorated the walls with pictures: a portrait of herself, a group picture of her family, and snapshots of several friends. Sam contributed the bearskin rugs, which he spread on the floor. Above the mantelpiece he hung the antlers of a prairie deer he had shot. Belle, who loved books, placed all the ones she had taken from her father's library after his death and lined them up on a shelf nailed to the wall.

Sam added another room to the cabin, along with a smokehouse for curing meat and a corncrib. Finally, he built a corral for his cattle and horses, which were then being pastured at his father's place.

Now everything was ready for Pearl, who was still living in Arkansas. Myra must have worried about how her daughter would accept this change from town life to a wilderness cabin. But Pearl took to her new home joyfully, delighting in the freedom it gave her. From the first she accepted Sam, whose last name Belle now gave her daughter so that it would match her own. Sam was different from anyone Pearl had ever known. He was quiet, soft-spoken, moving inconspicuously as a shadow. His penetrating dark eyes held a gentle kindness in their depth, a warmth that welcomed her. She began calling him Uncle Sam.

Pearl liked almost everything about him, especially the respectful attention he showed her mother and his protective concern for her. Unlike Jim Reed, he did not shirk the work necessary to make Youngers' Bend flourish. That first year, he and Belle cleared three acres of land, sowing most of it in corn. The rest became a vegetable garden. The family food supply was rounded out with game—prairie deer and turkey—which Sam shot in the wooded mountains. The Canadian River provided bass, catfish, and perch.

The first visitor from Belle's past to visit her at Youngers' Bend was the famous Jesse James. After a series of bold train holdups, a price of $10,000 was offered for his capture, dead or alive. One day he appeared unannounced on Belle's front porch. He had come to Youngers' Bend to hide from determined posses. Belle welcomed him joyfully, for he brought with him sweet and poignant memories of a past when she had courted so much danger to protect her beloved brother. Learning that James was a wanted man, she did not even tell Sam of their guest's identity for fear he might let something slip accidentally. Instead, she introduced him as Mr. Williams from Texas.

James spent two weeks with the Starrs. He and Belle exchanged stories of their exciting wartime adventures while Sam listened fascinated. It was only after James left that Belle told Sam who their guest was. Sam stared at her in awe. For a long while James had been his hero— a hero of mythical proportions. He could not believe that he and James had spent so much time talking to each other face-to-face.

It was the last visit Jesse James would ever make to Youngers' Bend. In April of 1882, sad news reached the Starrs. On the third of the month, James had been shot in the back by a false friend who was after the bounty. When the news got around that Jesse James had visited Belle Starr, it fed the rumors that had already attached themselves to her—the Civil War spy, the widow of a notorious outlaw Jim Reed, briefly the wife (or was it the mistress?) of gambler Bruce Younger, and now the wife

PROCLAMATION

OF THE

GOVERNOR OF MISSOURI!

REWARDS

FOR THE ARREST OF

Express and Train Robbers.

STATE OF MISSOURI,
EXECUTIVE DEPARTMENT.

WHEREAS, It has been made known to me, as the Governor of the State of Missouri, that certain parties, whose names are to me unknown, have confederated and banded themselves together for the purpose of committing robberies and other depredations within this State; and

WHEREAS, Said parties did, on or about the Eighth day of October, 1879, stop a train near Glendale, in the county of Jackson, in said State, and, with force and violence, take, steal and carry away the money and other express matter being carried thereon; and

WHEREAS, On the Fifteenth day of July, 1881, said parties and their confederates did stop a train upon the line of the Chicago, Rock Island and Pacific Railroad, near Winston, in the County of Daviess, in said State, and, with force and violence, take, steal, and carry away the money and other express matter being carried thereon, and, in perpetration of the robbery last aforesaid, the parties engaged therein did kill and murder one William Westfall, the conductor of the train, together with one John McCulloch, who was at the time in the employ of said company, then on said train; and

WHEREAS, Frank James and Jesse W. James stand indicted in the Circuit Court of said Daviess County, for the murder of John W. Sheets; and the parties engaged in the robberies and murders aforesaid have fled from justice and have absconded and secreted themselves:

NOW THEREFORE, in consideration of the premises, and in lieu of other rewards heretofore offered for the arrest or conviction of the parties aforesaid, or either of them, by any person or corporation, I, THOMAS T. CRITTENDEN, Governor of the State of Missouri, do hereby offer a reward of five thousand dollars ($5,000,00) for the arrest and conviction of each person participating, in either of the robberies or murders aforesaid, excepting the said Frank James and Jesse W. James; and for the arrest and delivery of said

FRANK JAMES and JESSE W. JAMES,

and each or either of them, to the sheriff of said Daviess County, I hereby offer a reward of ten thousand dollars, ($10,000,00) and for the conviction of either of the parties last aforesaid of participation in either of the murders or robberies above mentioned, I hereby offer a further reward of ten thousand dollars, ($10,000,00)

IN TESTIMONY WHEREOF, I have hereunto set my hand and caused to be affixed the Great Seal of the State of Missouri. Done

[SEAL] at the City of Jefferson on this 28th day of July, A. D. 1881.

THOS. T. CRITTENDEN.

By the Governor:
MICH'L K. McGRATH, Sec'y of State.

Notorious outlaw brothers Frank and Jesse James were wanted for several crimes, including this train robbery.

of the son of the notorious Cherokee Tom Starr.

As Belle was to write:

> On the Canadian River . . . I hoped to pass the
> remainder of my life in peace . . . For a short time
> I lived very happily with my little girl and hus-
> band. But it became noised about that I was a
> woman of notoriety from Texas and from that
> time on my home and actions have been severely
> criticized . . . My home became famous as an
> outlaw ranch long before I was visited by any of
> the boys who were friends of mine . . .

The damaging rumors to which Belle was alluding
might have died down if she had not given them fresh fuel
by her own behavior.

Chapter Eight

THE HOUSE OF CORRECTION

What began as a simple quarrel over a horse soon escalated into disaster for Belle and her husband. Belle and Sam were on the property of two brothers, John and Frank West. The brothers boarded horses on their ranch, and Belle wanted to discuss boarding some of hers there occasionally. As they talked, Belle noticed a horse running wild on the West property. Taking a liking to him, she asked to borrow the horse for two or three days to see how he rode. John told her the horse was not his to lend, since he belonged to another neighbor. But Belle, in the high-handed manner she had often displayed as a child, took the horse anyway, along with a mare that was owned by another rancher.

During the next few weeks, the owner of the horse tried repeatedly to get him back from Belle without any success. At last he went to Fort Smith and signed a complaint against the Starrs. A warrant was issued for their arrest, and a federal marshal with several deputies went to bring them in. Aware of the hot temper both Starrs had, the marshal played a trick on them. He and his deputies surprised Sam and overpowered him. They gagged him and tied him to a tree beside the trail. Then they hid and waited for Belle to come along.

When she arrived and saw Sam by the tree, she started toward him. Suddenly the waiting men sprang upon her, giving Belle no time to snatch one of the three or four pistols she was carrying under her skirt and the pannier on the horse. The lawmen confiscated her guns and subdued Belle, whose arms and legs were flailing in all directions. They brought her to the wagons they had concealed down the trail.

The wagons carried supplies for the long trip to Fort Smith, where Belle and Sam would go for trial. The marshal expected to be on the road at least six weeks, collecting other prisoners along the way. One wagon held housekeeping articles, another tents for camping. A third was reserved for the prisoners. Belle, the only woman prisoner, was placed in the supply wagon by herself. There she sat, steaming with fury amidst a collection of silverware, plates, cups, pots, pans and food supplies. She began to grab at anything she could lay her hands on. One after the other, she tossed them out of the wagon to go crashing and banging down the road.

In the racket of clattering hooves and creaking wagons, the deputies never realized what Belle was doing until they came to the next stop and the cooks started to prepare a meal. Then they discovered half their cooking utensils were missing. But still mindful that Belle was a woman deserving of respect, the men kept their patience, until one day things reached a climax.

The wagons had made a routine stop at noon to allow the marshal and his deputies to go off after some other prisoners, leaving the camp under a skeleton guard. The camp cooks had prepared lunch, and Belle, who had been given a tent of her own, was sitting in it eating her meal when a sudden gust of wind surged against the tent's flap, blowing it open.

Through the gap Belle saw the guard sitting with his back to her, his gun in its holster riding on his hip. She darted forward, snatched the gun out and fired it into the air. The man whirled around. His face blanched, his mouth gaped. Then he skittered off, rushing around the camp with Belle charging after him and firing her pistol. *Pop, pop, pop* sounded the gun. The guard was sure Belle meant to kill him, not knowing she was a crack shot and could have brought him down with a single bullet. She was only trying to terrify the other guards into fleeing so that she could free all the prisoners and escape with Sam.

The marshal had completed his roundup of prisoners and was returning when he heard the gun shots. He and his men rushed to the camp, guns leveled, in time to stop Belle. After that, Belle was chained for the rest of the trip. Because of her delaying tactics, the trip had taken eight weeks instead of six to reach Fort Smith. As the humiliating chains were removed, Belle vowed that she would never again be caught in such an embarrassing situation.

Once at Fort Smith, the rest was routine. A grand jury indicted Sam and Belle and the trial was set for February 15, 1883. Until then, Sam and Belle were released to Tom Starr, who posted a promissory note listing his assets as proof he could cover the $1,000 bail in case the couple fled.

Judge Isaac Charles Parker was going to preside over Sam and Belle's trial. In 1875, President Ulysses S. Grant had appointed Judge Parker to the thankless job of cleaning up the mess in the Fort Smith federal court, as well as putting an end to the rash of criminals who were plaguing the Indian Territory. To avoid long, drawn out appeals that were tying up the local judicial system, Judge Parker was given full authority over those who came before him for trial. When the jury brought in the verdict, Judge Parker would pronounce a sentence that was immediately carried out. The most drastic punishment was hanging, which was reserved for rape and murder.

During his first court session, Judge Parker ordered the hanging of six men. A giant gallows capable of hanging as many as twelve men at once was built. The hanging of the first six men was a public spectacle, and families came from miles around to witness it. In the years to come, there would be so many of these group hangings that Judge Parker earned the title of the Hanging Judge.

As the Starr trial opened, the courtroom quickly filled

with excited spectators. A local paper, drawing on all the myths and rumors floating around Belle's head, covered the story with these words: "The very idea of a woman being charged with an offense of this kind and that she was the leader of a band of horse thieves and wielding a power over them as their queen and guiding spirit, was sufficient to fill the courtroom with spectators."

Throughout the trial, Belle sat up straight, staring at Judge Parker. Now and then she would scribble a hasty note and pass it to her lawyer. She followed the proceedings with keen interest. On the other hand, Sam showed no interest at all. He sat with his head bowed like a trapped animal. On one occasion, thinking that he was ignorant because he was a Native American, the supercilious prosecutor decided to have some fun at Sam's expense. Using intricate legal terms, he tripped Sam up repeatedly. Whenever Sam stumbled over the unfamiliar phrases, the prosecutor would shrug and sneer knowingly at the jury.

Belle was furious. It was all she could do to keep from leaping up and attacking the arrogant prosecutor. She managed to keep herself in hand, however, expressing her anger only by such a malignant stare that, as one reporter put it, "If looks had been killing, the prosecutor would have dropped in his tracks."

The trial was soon over. Dozens of witnesses appeared for the prosecution, but only a handful for the defense. The most important defense witness was a man named Russell Childs who, Belle claimed, had inadvertently included the two horses in a batch he had just bought from her. Now she was unable to locate him. Unfortunately, Childs turned out to be a notorious horse thief who was hiding out in Texas.

The most damning testimony came from John West, who kept insisting that he had told Belle the two horses were not his to lend and she had taken them anyway and never returned them.

It did not take long for the jury to reach a guilty verdict. The fate of Belle and Sam Starr lay in the hands of the Hanging Judge. Though he was not likely to hang them, he could give them both stiff prison sentences.

On March 8, 1883, Belle and Sam Starr were brought before Judge Parker for sentencing. Sam faced the judge, his face dark with the resignation and despair his people had been suffering ever since the arrival of the Europeans. But Belle stood straight and tall beside him, her accusing stare fastened unflinchingly on the judge.

Judge Parker returned her gaze reprovingly. But his sentence was surprisingly lenient. He sentenced Sam to one year in the House of Correction at Detroit, Michigan. He gave Belle two six month terms in the same House, to be served one after the other. But with good behavior, he told them, they could cut their sentences to nine months each. He concluded with the advice that the Starrs should try to become decent citizens.

Until transportation to Detroit arrived, Belle and Sam were lodged in the local jail in the basement of the courthouse. There on March 18, the eve of her departure, Belle wrote a farewell letter to her daughter, whom she had already sent to live with her friends the McLaughlins in Kansas. She wrote: ". . . I shall be away from you a few months, baby, and have only this consolation to offer you that never again will I be placed in such humiliating circumstances . . ." Then, putting the best light on the situation, she explained that the House of Correction was not a penitentiary but a pleasant place in fine surroundings: "There I can have my education renewed and I stand really in need of it. Sam will have to attend school and I think it is the best thing could ever happen to him . . ."

On March 19, Belle and Sam were escorted to a railroad prison car at the Fort Smith depot to take them to Detroit. After two days of travel, they entered the House of Correction and began their sentences. Sam was offered an education but refused it, still wanting nothing to do with the hated white man's culture. He preferred instead to spend his time at hard physical labor.

Belle was given the same light work that other female prisoners did—fastening cane slats across the seats of chair frames. In her free time, Belle joined some of the women who were interested in getting an education. But she soon realized that she already knew the lessons being taught. So instead she started helping to tutor the others.

The matron of the women's division, an educated person herself, was delighted to have Belle's help. Soon the two women became good friends, often having long discussions on their favorite topic—current literature. The warden of the House of Correction was also pleased to have an educated woman there. It was rumored that he enlisted Belle to tutor his children in French and music. He also relaxed the rules enough to let her have pen, ink and paper to write an article about the House of Correction and her autobiography. But neither of these projects has ever been found.

Chapter Nine

BELLE STARR'S REWARD

Belle and Sam's imprisonment was shortened to nine months, which came to an end at Christmas-time. Upon his release, Sam went directly to Youngers' Bend, while Belle went to Rich Hill, where she planned to spend the holidays with her children and the Reed relatives. Eddie, who was almost thirteen by this time, had grown tired of humdrum country life and had already left for grandmother Eliza's home in Dallas. Pearl, who had left the McLaughlins to be with the Reeds, was waiting eagerly for her mother. Belle had put on weight during her stay at the House of Correction, but Pearl scarcely noticed it. She wanted to introduce Belle to her new friend, a girl her own age, fifteen-year-old Mabel Harrison.

Mabel had been living with the Reeds ever since she was seven years old, when a gang of desperadoes had broken into her home and murdered both her parents in front of her. Seeing the attachment between the two girls, Belle invited Mabel to accompany them to Youngers' Bend. Following the Christmas holidays, the three set off at once.

They found Youngers' Bend flourishing. Tom Starr had faithfully kept up the property. The vegetable garden had been freshly plowed, ready for the spring planting. The cows had been fed and milked daily and were in fine condition. The two cats the family had left behind had multiplied into twenty-one kittens of all sizes and colors that sent Belle and the girls into gales of laughter.

The family quickly settled into familiar routines. The girls attended the local school together. They were welcomed by the other students, most of whom were members of the extended Starr clan. In their free time, the two took long horseback rides, exchanging secrets with each other, growing closer and closer with each passing day.

The girls enjoyed preparing meals for the family while Belle, who hated cooking except for candy-making, worked outside, a job she had liked from the days on her father's farm in Scyene. She planted vegetables as a matter of course. But she was most interested in her flower garden. Whenever she took a trip, she would collect young plants, roots, and seeds along the way to plant in her garden at home. Soon the beds around the cabin were a riot of color.

Belle made frequent trips to satisfy her gadabout instincts. She would make a sudden decision to take to the road, pack her clothes and food supplies, hitch the horses to one of the farm wagons, and be off for several days of visiting with friends and relatives in Arkansas, Missouri, or Kansas. She usually took Pearl with her on these jaunts, leaving Sam in charge of Mabel and Eddie, who had now joined the family.

But Belle spent most of her time at Youngers' Bend. She soon became known in the neighborhood for her concern about families in need. Let illness strike and Belle would be there, often with an overnight bag, to take charge of things—nursing the sick, cooking, washing, tending to the children. Children loved to see her come because she always entertained them with so many exciting stories.

Belle's concern for her neighbors went beyond petty differences. Though she and her husband were still angry with John West for his testimony against them at the trial, it did not stop Belle from rushing to the West home to help John's wife through a difficult childbirth. The women whom Belle helped had never seen her tough side. When they heard her criticized, they would come to her defense, describing her as a soft-spoken, genteel lady who was always there for them.

But Belle had another side, one that she kept carefully under control throughout that quiet year. It was the side that preferred the company of men to that of most women. She enjoyed matching men in sharp conversation, in riding and shooting skills, and in daredevil action. Most of all, she admired the outlaws because they dared defy the law to live life as they chose. Sam's outlaw mates were always warmly welcomed at the cabin, as were Belle's old guerrilla friends whenever they dropped by for a visit.

But Belle did not need a lot of company. She loved books and spent hours reading. The few close women friends she had were educated like herself, and Belle treasured their visits because she could discuss literature and music with them intelligently. But such women were scarce in Belle's neighborhood. She found most of the women living there to be boring. Whenever she saw one of them approaching the cabin for what she knew would be a long, empty conversation, she would grab a book and a pillow and dash off to hide in one of the farm wagons. There, hidden from sight, she would settle down to read.

"Why, Mama," Pearl would remonstrate, leaning into the wagon, "Mrs. So and So doesn't know what to think. You surely aren't going to hide out here all day."

Belle would answer, "All she can talk about is pumpkins and babies. I can't stand such gab."

Belle's other love was music. Whenever she visited a friend who had a piano, she could not keep away from it. At the least encouragement she would sit down and play for hours. Some people claimed that Belle went to Fort Smith just for the chance to visit saloons or gambling halls where there were pianos and sit for hours playing them. What Belle really yearned for was a piano of her own, not just for herself, but for Pearl. Belle was already tutoring her daughter in French and Latin, subjects she was not getting at school. But she felt Pearl's education would be incomplete unless she could play the piano well.

One day during a visit to Fort Smith, Belle had a stroke of luck. Riding down a city street, she chanced upon two men standing beside a large crate containing a piano. Belle stopped to talk to them and found out that one of the men, a Choctaw named Icsam Perry, had just bought the piano from a pioneer family who told him it was almost new. A short time before Belle arrived, the family had been passing through Fort Smith on the way to Texas. Their covered wagon was piled high with household goods, among them the piano. The hungry children were crying for food. The father was desperate. He had no money for food. Did the Choctaw know of anyone who would buy the piano?

Perry had only fifty dollars, which his neighbors in the town of Whitefield had given him to purchase some needed supplies in Fort Smith. Without thinking, he had handed the money over to the desperate father, who unloaded the piano and left. Now the Choctaw was afraid to show up at home empty handed. How could he explain that in a moment of compassion he had given away their money to a stranger passing through?

Belle swept her fingers up and down the black and white piano keys and found they were in tune. Mindful of her problems with the borrowed horse, she asked Perry for a bill of sale to make sure he owned the piano. Perry pulled out some crumpled papers from his pocket and handed them to Belle. She looked them over, then opened her purse, took out $50 and handed it to Perry, warning him to get the supplies he had been sent to buy and then "skin for home."

Next she turned to the man who had been standing beside Perry and whom she recognized as a freighter. She handed him another fifty dollars to haul the piano to Youngers' Bend.

As soon as the piano arrived and was uncrated in the living room, Belle contacted an itinerant music teacher named Charley Williams and asked him to come by to give Pearl and Eddie music lessons. Eddie turned out to have some talent, but did not care for music. Pearl wanted desperately to play and tried very hard, practicing for hours. But she had little talent and under the pressure she became ill with the flu. It was such a severe attack that Belle sent a Cherokee messenger to the nearest town to fetch a doctor.

After that, the piano lessons were stopped and the family resumed its laid-back life. Everything ran along smoothly because Eddie as well as Pearl had accepted Sam wholeheartedly. Though usually rambunctious, Eddie warmed to the quiet, soft-spoken Cherokee who took him out on hunting trips, teaching the boy how to track down game and kill it with one skillfully placed shot.

As December arrived, Belle could look back with satisfaction on the year just passed. She had kept her promise to Pearl not to get entangled in any more embarrassing situations. Then one day close to Christmas, at the stroke of noon, there came an urgent knock on the door that would shatter the well-earned tranquility of the family living in the little cabin at Youngers' Bend.

Chapter Ten

THE ONE-EYED MARE

The man filling the doorway of the Starr cabin was sturdily built. His craggy face, bronzed by the sun, bristled with a yellowish mustache. The top of one ear was missing. He was well dressed in a heavy winter coat, cashmere pants, and low boots.

Belle recognized him as John Middleton, a notorious horse thief. He explained that he had just killed the sheriff of Lamar County, Texas, and was now running for his life. He had managed to get to Indian Territory and had made his way to Youngers' Bend, expecting Belle to help him. He needed her help because the Texas authorities had appealed to John West, who was now a police officer, to help them. West had been guiding the Texans through the wilderness around Youngers' Bend, but so far without success. In the dead of winter, the Texans had gone home, leaving their warrant with John West, who promised to keep up the search with his usual dogged persistence.

With their resentment against John West still high,

Middleton won the help of both Belle and Sam. From Christmas Day to April, Middleton hid at Younger's Bend. Though at the beginning Sam did not know Middleton, he quickly warmed to him and the two became good friends. That was lucky for the outlaw because Sam knew the wilderness around Youngers' Bend like nobody else. He was kept busy finding new hiding places for their guest as John West and his deputies scoured the area.

The situation grew more tense when spring came, bringing pleasant weather and the return of the Texas lawmen. One day, John West and his men burst into the Starr cabin, hoping to surprise Middleton there. All they found was Belle, who greeted them, her hand on the six-shooter strapped to her waist. She began scolding them for their lack of manners. Then in the midst of her tirade she burst into wild, hysterical laughter, taunting them with their inability to capture a lone fugitive.

The posse left, but their invasion into a private home had alarmed the Starrs and Middleton. They became even more worried when Cherokee informers dropped by to tell them that the lawmen were beginning to seal off every exit point from the Bend. If Middleton did not get away soon, he would become trapped, and it would be only a matter of time before they flushed him out.

It was Belle who came up with a plan. She and Pearl would make one of their frequent trips to Arkansas. As usual, they would travel by covered wagon, camping along the way. This would enable them to smuggle Middleton out without arousing suspicion. They brought out the wagon and made a big show of packing it in case hidden spies were watching. When they were finished, they tied their favorite riding horses behind the wagon, as they always did on trips so that wherever they stopped they could go horseback riding.

After everything was ready, Middleton stole into the wagon and hid under some covers, his shotgun beside him. Then Belle and Pearl climbed onto the front seat beside Frank, their driver. They set off, Sam and Eddie accompanying them on horseback.

The plan was simple. Traveling by day and camping by night, the wagon would take several days to get clear of the trap the posse was setting for Middleton. Then Pearl would lend him her horse while Belle would lend him the fancy saddle she had just bought for Pearl, along with her own treasured ivory-handled Colt. Middleton would then ride off to freedom. Once in Arkansas, he would leave the horse, bridle, and gun at a predetermined spot to be picked up later by Sam and Belle.

Things went very well until the last lap of the journey, when Middleton and Pearl got into a nasty quarrel—so nasty that when they reached Middleton's last stop, Pearl refused to lend him her horse. She was so adamant about it that Belle told Middleton to hide in some nearby woods while she located another horse for him. A short while later, she came upon a rancher named Fayette Barnett, who was out looking for some of his stray cows. When Belle explained her problem, he promised to get a horse for her. He was gone only a short while. When he came back he had a mare in tow. Barnett never told Belle the mare did not belong to him. He had just stolen it from another rancher named Albert G. McCarty.

The mare was a sorry sight. Her feet were unshod and she was blind in one eye. But she would have to do. Belle asked Eddie and Sam to take the mare to Middleton. When Middleton saw the horse he lost his temper at her sorry appearance. But he knew there was no time to look for another. Cursing the mare, which was not worth the fifty dollars Barnett wanted for her, Middleton paid and Barnett left.

Middleton placed Pearl's saddle on the horse and attached the holster containing Belle's revolver to it. Then, still cursing, he mounted the mare and was off, traveling as fast as the broken-down animal could carry him. Meanwhile, Eddie and Sam rode back to Youngers' Bend, while Belle and Pearl continued their trip to visit friends in Arkansas.

Four days later, on May 7, a Choctaw spotted a one-eyed mare in a thicket of brush by the bank of the Arkansas River, just twenty-five miles from Fort Smith. The mare was covered with drying mud. On its back was Pearl's expensive saddle and the holster carrying Belle's Colt.

The man immediately began searching for the rider of

the mare. Eventually John Middleton's body was found downstream. He had tried to swim across the swift-running river but had been separated from the mare and swept away by the current. John West was notified and came at once. He identified the body and had it buried on the spot.

When John West recognized Pearl's fancy saddle and Belle's famous Colt revolver, he set off in search of Belle to question her. He found her covered wagon at Dardanelle, Arkansas, where she and Pearl were camping. He entered the wagon and began rummaging around for some more evidence that would tie Belle to Middleton. In his search, he came upon a locked trunk and started to break it open. He was confronted by a furious Belle. Eyes blazing, she flung herself between him and her trunk and defied him to open it.

West stared down the barrel of her gun leveled at his head and backed out of the wagon. Belle watched as he left. She had won this victory, but she knew it was only a small one. She had heard from West that Middleton was dead, and that the one-eyed mare had been found still carrying Pearl's saddle and her prize Colt. She knew she was in trouble and should be back at Youngers' Bend handling things from there. So she and Pearl broke off their vacation and headed for home.

Already newspapers had gotten hold of the story and were making the most of it. Every day they came up with new theories: Belle was Middleton's mistress; she was eloping with him when the accident occurred. Other old rumors that Belle had worked so hard to dispel were back again, more fantastic than ever. Some claimed Belle was the queen of a thriving gang of cattle thieves, with stations located at intervals along the route from Kansas to Arkansas to Texas. At these stations, stolen cattle were sold or exchanged. Other rumors described the lookouts Belle was stationing in the caves that pocked the cliff face at Youngers' Bend. From there the lookouts spied on travelers. If any of them were carrying valuable merchandise, the hidden spies would send a signal to waiting gangs below who would pounce on the traveler, kill him, and steal his possessions. The stories claimed Belle used the caves to stash stolen goods.

Belle was dismayed that her efforts to lead a quiet life had been ruined. To make matters worse, she learned that Barnett had stolen the one-eyed mare from McCarty. If the owner signed a complaint against her, she could expect the Wests to show up with a warrant for her arrest on the charge of larceny.

As if this were not enough, on June 15, 1885, Sam was accused of being one of three masked men who robbed the United States mail wagon during its run through the Cherokee Nation. There was not any proof that could link Sam to the raid, so no formal complaint had been made. But who could tell what the future would bring with the West brothers determined to haul Sam in for one reason or another?

On top of everything, Belle suddenly found herself facing another pressing problem. Her daughter Pearl, now seventeen, had been seeing a great deal of a young classmate named Robert McClure. Belle had seen him at various dances she and Pearl had attended but had taken little notice of him. On this day, she had to notice him because he had come to ask Belle for her daughter's hand in marriage.

Belle was shocked. The McClure family was certainly not wealthy enough to match Belle's idea of a proper husband for Pearl. She responded harshly to the young man's request, telling him that she would never give her consent to her daughter's marriage to anyone who did not have at least $25,000 in the bank.

Crestfallen, young McClure replied that never in a million years would he have that much money and left. Belle was not content with leaving it at that. She felt she had to put a definite end to the romance. Without saying a word to Pearl about the young man's proposal, she asked her daughter if she would like to pay another visit to her cousins in Arkansas. Pearl, who expected to be gone only a couple of weeks, jumped at the idea. The two set out for Arkansas to visit the Reed relatives. Belle dropped Pearl off there and returned to Youngers' Bend.

As soon as she got home, Belle sat down and wrote a letter. It began with a lot of farewells scrawled across the page. The "farewells" were followed with, "I was married last Thursday to a rich man who has lots of stock and

$25,000 in the bank; so you see I have got that money just as mama said."

Belle signed the letter "*PEARL.*"

Belle posted the letter and, with Pearl safely stranded far from home, she waited to see what would happen. As she had hoped, McClure accepted the letter as genuine and was overwhelmed by a sense of betrayal and loss. He asked himself how Pearl could desert him for the sake of money after they had exchanged promises of undying love. And how could she dismiss him with such a cold, cruel letter, not even bothering to talk to him face-to-face? He left town and soon married another young woman.

When Belle got this news she brought Pearl back to Youngers' Bend. Pearl learned of her boyfriend's sudden marriage and wondered, brokenhearted and bewildered, how he could have deserted her after promising her undying love.

Seeing her daughter's unhappiness may have made Belle sad, but certainly she did not feel guilty for meddling in her life. Perhaps she remembered all too vividly how she had given her undying love to a penniless, teenaged Jim Reed and how he had betrayed her.

Chapter Eleven

BELLE HANDLES THINGS

The holiday season of 1885-86 was an uneasy time for the Starrs. They knew that the Wests were still investigating the circumstances surrounding the theft of the one-eyed mare and that the animal had been traced to its owner, Albert McCarty. Belle was sure that when McCarty learned that her revolver and Pearl's fancy saddle had been found on the horse's back, he would assume she was the thief and would sign a complaint against her. In mid-January, she heard that the warrant she had been dreading had been issued and knew West would be on his way to arrest her. She had no intention of being dragged to Fort Smith in disgrace as had happened to her the last time.

Belle decided to avoid being served the warrant by going to Fort Smith ahead of its arrival. On January 21, she rode into town and turned herself in to the United States marshal. On February 8, she pleaded not guilty and put in a request for witnesses who could testify on her behalf. Judge Parker set the trial for the next session of federal court in September.

Belle posted her own bail and set off again for Youngers' Bend. Along the way she paid a visit to Barnett, the real culprit. She reminded him quietly that she was innocent and could prove it. Barnett promised nervously that he would help her in every way he could, including paying her lawyers' fees.

Satisfied with Barnett's promise, Belle continued on home to find that Sam was now in trouble. No complaint had been made about the first U.S. mail robbery, but the three men had struck again, this time in a store and post office in the town of Blaine. A complaint was sworn against Sam. He was indicted, though still with no proof of his guilt, and a warrant was issued for him.

Then on February 27, Sam was accused of being one of three men who broke into the house of a farmer named Wilse Farrill who lived near Fort Smith, the robbers coming away with a mere forty dollars. Though none of the men could be positively identified, suspicion again fell on Sam and another warrant was issued. With two warrants out for Sam, Youngers' Bend began to swarm with lawmen. It was all Belle and Pearl could do to keep him out of their clutches.

At one point, an exasperated John West appealed to Belle to get her husband to give himself up voluntarily. Belle lashed out at him. She told him that the charges against her husband were just hearsay. There was no real proof that he had committed any of the acts charged against him. She was afraid that if he gave himself up to the tribal police, he would be condemned and shot on the spot by the Choctaw chiefs who still carried a grudge against his father and wanted revenge.

From then on, it was war between the Wests and Belle. Belle's chief weapon was not her gun but her sharp-tongued ridicule of the Wests and their posses. One popular story described such an incident in the ongoing tug of war.

One morning, Belle met the posse halfway up the narrow trail that led to Youngers' Bend. Instead of lashing out at them, Belle greeted them hospitably. She told them they looked tired and hungry and wanted to know if they would like her to whip up some lunch for them. The men responded gratefully, following Belle through the canyon at a leisurely pace. By the time they reached the compound around the cabin, Sam, who had been at home at the time, had slipped away into the nearby woods.

While the men watered their horses, Belle began preparing a stew. By the time the men sat down to it, the odors were rich and tantalizing. The men began to eat, proclaiming the stew delicious. When they were done, they settled back for a leisurely smoke. During the course of their conversation, Belle asked them if they could guess what they had just eaten. When they could not, she responded, "Well, that was an old rattlesnake I killed this morning. Now go and puke it up."

But the rattlesnake stew was not enough to shame off the Wests. It only made them angrier. In early March,

John West responded by leading a posse made up of Cherokee and Choctaws back to the Starr cabin, where they burst in on Sam, who was entertaining some of his outlaw friends. Though surprised, they all managed to slip away like shadows, leaving the clumsy posse empty handed.

By this time, a desperate John West conceived a plan to force Sam into the open. Knowing the protective instincts of most Cherokee men toward their women, he planned to flush out Sam by arresting Belle. He filed a complaint against her based on the rumors floating around naming her as the mastermind behind the Farrill house break-in, as well as the leader of the raid itself. Warrant in hand the two-man posse set out from Fort Smith to arrest Belle.

It was mid-May and close to dusk when the posse arrived at Youngers' Bend. Sam and Belle were both at home. Pearl, who was outside, saw the men and rushed in to warn of their approach. Sam slipped away, but Belle held her ground. She met the posse at the door and broke into derisive laughter at their appearance. Why, she asked, were their teeth chattering? And why were their clothes so rumpled and their trouser knees so muddy? Could it possibly be that they had crawled on their hands and knees to surprise and capture her before she fired a shot at them?

But Belle, for all her sarcastic jokes, had had enough of games. She told the men there was no need for violence.

She would accompany them peaceably to Fort Smith. With this, she went out and mounted her horse. Pearl joined her, planning to ride with her mother for a while.

The little group set out on the narrow trail that led through the canyon. As the echoes of the horses' hooves clattered against the canyon walls, the posse members held their breath. Was Sam the crack shot somewhere out there waiting with his rifle?

Belle and Pearl did not need to wonder. They knew he was. Their sharp eyes detected his shadow flitting in and out silently among the trees. All the while, he carried his rifle ready, his target the hated lawmen.

Every time Sam seemed to have a clear shot at one of the men, Belle or Pearl would ride between the leveled gun and its target. Both women knew that all it would take was one shot from the rifle to bring a charge of murder against Sam.

Once the posse was clear of the snaky trail, the landscape widened and they were free from danger. Pearl turned back and Belle continued on to Fort Smith. While Belle was in the town, she was approached by a lawyer who was representing a condemned Cherokee man named Blue Duck. A jury had convicted him of murder, and Judge Parker had sentenced him to hang. In a desperate move to save his client's life, the lawyer was asking a number of influential people to intercede with the judge on Blue Duck's behalf. Belle was one of these people. Despite the wild rumors surrounding her, she still com-

Belle had her portrait taken with her friend Blue Duck during her trial at Fort Smith.
(Fred S. Barde College, Courtesy of the Archives & Manuscripts Division of the Oklahoma Historical Society, 4631.)

manded a great deal of respect in the area, especially from the judge. The lawyer hoped that a picture of Blue Duck and Belle together would impress the judge.

Belle also sat for another photograph, this one showing her in a riding costume, sitting sidesaddle on a horse. The photograph was taken to illustrate an article that was being written about her by a renowned reporter, Albert A. Powe. He was the first newsman to whom Belle had ever given an interview; she knew how writers were prone to distort the truth. But this man promised to stick to the facts she gave him. And because of his reputation for honesty, she decided to trust him, hoping that his article would dispel the lurid rumors swirling around her.

Two weeks after returning to Youngers' Bend, Belle went back to Fort Smith for her trial on the Farrill house break-in. By this time the article had appeared in a number of southwestern newspapers, creating a great stir. It was a long article purporting to tell the true story of Belle's life. But instead of sticking to her factual account, Powe embellished it with many half-truths, downright lies, and fanciful exaggerations. Belle's mother had sent her a copy of the offensive article, which had appeared in a Dallas newspaper.

As Belle entered the lobby of the Fort Smith courthouse, she spotted Powe sitting behind a railing where the deputies on duty were stationed. Passing close to the railing, Belle stared at the scrawny reporter, his eyes glinting behind his huge spectacles, avid for another sensational story. Quick as a tiger's pounce, Belle's long arm darted out. A muscular hand grabbed the newsman by the scruff of his neck and dragged him over the railing. Then, lifting her riding quirt, Belle gave him a whipping, lash after lash, for the lies he had told. Finally she pushed him aside contemptuously and strode calmly into the courtroom where the judge was waiting.

He listened to a few of the prosecution witnesses but refrained from calling on Belle's defenders, who were ready to swear they had seen her at a dance the night of the break-in. Instead, he dismissed the whole case, saying it was ridiculous and not worthy of the court's time. Now Belle had only one charge against her, that of stealing the one-eyed mare. With Barnett's promised help, she knew that charge, too, would give her no problems.

Chapter Twelve

ENDINGS

Unknown to Belle, another problem was shaping up, one that could not be resolved in a court of law. In the spring of 1886, Bob McClure returned to the vicinity of Youngers' Bend. When he arrived and found that Pearl was unmarried, he must have realized the cruel trick Belle had played on him. He decided to tell Pearl about it. But when he tried to approach her, she refused even to greet him and passed with a disdainful tilt of her head.

Bob was persistent. In mid-July, at a community picnic, he managed to catch hold of Pearl's hand and draw her aside. In a low voice he began telling her about his visit to Belle, how she had refused to consent to their marriage and how shortly afterward he had received a letter signed "Pearl" telling him that she had married a rich man.

Pearl listened in growing shock as she began to realize the cruel truth: Bob had never deserted her. In a trembling voice, he described his own heartbreak and hurt at receiving that cold, unfeeling letter, and she understood at last the despair and sense of betrayal that had sent him into the arms of another woman.

On the crowded picnic grounds, intimate talk was impossible. The couple agreed to meet again in private. They chose a secret spot in Youngers' Bend. There, in the quiet beneath the sheltering trees, they clung to each other. Nothing had changed. The old love was there, as passionate and stronger than ever. Bob began to plead with Pearl for another chance. He told her he could try for an annulment or get a divorce. Something would be worked out and they could be together at last.

After thinking it over, Pearl refused his offer. Her pride had been too deeply hurt by his quick marriage. She told herself that if he had truly believed in her love for him, he would have questioned that cold, cruel letter, or at least have checked it out. If he could not stand up against one brief assault by her mother, how would he be able to face a continual barrage of attacks? Pearl knew only too well the sudden bursts of fury her mother displayed when crossed.

Clinging tightly to Bob, she told him all the reasons why this had to be their last visit. They could never be together again. There in the quiet glade, with only silent trees to watch, they kissed in tears and embraced.

The time for parting had come. There is no record that they ever spoke to or even saw each other again. But Pearl was left with one lasting memento of her passionate meeting with Bob McClure. A month or two later she confided to Mabel that she was pregnant, but her mother must never know. Faithful Mabel promised to keep as silent as the trees.

In September, an unsuspecting Belle set off for Fort Smith for her scheduled trial in the case of the one-eyed mare. While she was there, she received some terrible news from Youngers' Bend. The dogged stalking of the West brothers had finally succeeded. Frank West and his posse had surprised Sam as he was riding Belle's favorite mare, Venus, through their cornfields.

Frank's right-hand man suggested that they divide the posse into two groups that would close in on Sam from opposite sides, trapping him. But Frank was afraid that Sam might slip away as he had done so many times before. Frank raised his revolver and fired repeatedly at Sam's back. Sam cried out in pain and shock, bending backward as he groped for the saddle horn. A second bullet struck Sam in the side. A third hit the mare. She let out a scream and, throwing Sam, fell over dead. Sam hit the ground with full force. He rolled over and lay still beside the body of the mare.

Frank and his deputies rushed up. A pool of blood was forming under Sam's head where the bullet had struck. Blood was also dripping from his side, where the other bullet had found its mark. Seeing Sam's unmoving body, Frank suddenly began to regret his rash attack. He knew he had not followed correct police procedure but had fired at Sam's back without first identifying himself or giving Sam a chance to surrender. If Sam were to die, Frank would find himself in serious trouble with the law. He had to get a doctor as quickly as possible.

Leaving two members of his posse behind to stand guard over Sam, Frank set off with his deputy for the nearest farmhouse. He planned to get a wagon to bring Sam in so that his wounds could be properly dressed and everything done to keep him alive.

The two men left in charge of Sam decided to move him away from the cornfield and into the brush so that he would be out of sight of any passersby, especially members of the hostile Starr family.

Unknown to the men, Sam had regained consciousness. Watching through half-closed lids, he saw them put down their Winchesters so they could lift him. As they bent over him, Sam snatched a pistol from the holster of one of the men. Struggling to his feet with the pistol leveled at his captors, Sam disarmed them of all their weapons and threw them one after another as far as he could into the cornfield. Then, after mounting one of the horses and chasing away the other, he rode off with a last warning: "Tell Frank West he pay for killing Belle's mare."

Belle heard the story in Fort Smith. Helpless to go to her husband's side, she checked daily for the latest news about him—how he had managed to ride away despite his dangerous loss of blood, how the police were vainly searching for him. Belle knew exactly where her injured husband was—in the home of one of his brothers who always sheltered Sam when he was in trouble. She had to get home to him. Impatiently, she waited for her trial to end, and when it finally did, with an acquittal, she rushed home to find Sam at his brother's home, lingering between life and death. She took over nursing him, and gradually his wounds began to heal. As he convalesced, Belle continued urging him to sidestep the Wests and their posses and give himself directly to the U.S. marshal. She explained that he would fare better under the white man's law than under cruel Choctaw laws. And since there was no real proof that any of the accusations against him were true, he would likely be acquitted of all of them.

At last, Sam agreed to Belle's plan, and she quickly set about putting it into action. First she notified Deputy Tyner Hughes of Sam's decision. On October 4, the deputy arrived to take Sam into custody and out of the hands of the vengeful Choctaw and the determined Wests. Once in Fort Smith, Sam was indicted. His bail was set at $1,000. Belle had already arranged for this also, getting one half from a friend of the Starrs and the other half from a relative of the Reeds.

Now that Sam was free, protected by the powerful United States government, he and Belle decided to stay in Fort Smith to attend the Seventh Annual Fair of Western Arkansas. When Judge Parker learned of this, he asked Belle if she would play the part of an outlaw holding up a stagecoach in which he would play a passenger. According to a news item in a local paper, Belle performed the mock holdup with "exceeding verve." Belle and Sam also took part in several riding and shooting exhibitions. Belle, as always, proved herself the best of the lot in target shooting and acrobatic stunts that she performed on her galloping horse.

Belle was pleased to see Sam's lightheartedness during the five days of the fair. But when they were over, Sam was jolted back into reality. His father, Tom, was being held in jail for selling liquor in Indian Territory. Sam and Belle, who had been helped so many times by the old man, tried to hire Sam's lawyer to defend him. But Tom refused their offer. Instead he pleaded guilty and accepted Judge Parker's sentence: a year and a half at the Southern Illinois penitentiary. On November 27, Tom Starr left for prison and Sam and Belle returned to Youngers' Bend.

The lighthearted spirit in which Sam had enjoyed his first taste of real freedom in months was gone. Dejected and bitter about his father's sentence, he blamed most of the Starr troubles on the Wests. But Christmas was nearing, and Belle remembered how Sam had always enjoyed the holiday parties. One of the biggest was Lucy Surratt's Christmas dance, which she held every year at her house. This year the date was set for December 17, a Friday night. Eddie and Pearl, who called Mrs. Surratt "Aunt Lucy," also looked forward to this party every year. Perhaps it would lift Sam's spirits again.

The evening of the party, Belle and her family dressed in their best and set out on horseback for the Surratt home. A steady rain had been falling all day, turning the road into a muddy morass, and a freezing drizzle was still falling. At the foot of the low hill on which the Surratt home stood, the four stopped in an elm grove. There the Surratts had laid a large log fire to warm partygoers before they had to make the last steep climb up the hill. Already a group was gathered around the comforting blaze. The Starrs stopped only long enough to warm themselves and exchange a few greetings. Then they set off up the hill for the party.

As they approached, they realized that it did not sound as though the party was off to a good start. The music was thin, the dancers listless. As soon as the Starrs entered the ballroom they saw that a lone fiddler was providing the music. And though he was the well known Arvil B. Cole, he could not provide enough volume to the music to inspire the dancers.

When Cole saw Belle, he rushed to her. The guitarist who usually accompanied him had drunk too much, he explained. Now he was out cold. Would Belle accompany him on Mrs. Surratt's pedal organ?

Belle needed no encouragement. She sat down at the organ and was soon pounding out the sonorous strains of "Billy in the Low Ground," with Cole accompanying her on his lively fiddle. The party exploded into a stamping, whirling kaleidoscope of sound and color. Eddie and

Pearl joined the others, whirling, stamping, clapping, shouting in riotous Western style. Only Sam remained somber, sitting beside the open door next to his wife at the organ, hand on his revolver.

Down below, a late arrival had just stopped to warm his hands at the fire—Frank West. Everyone there knew the bad feeling between Frank and Sam. And some of the men, wanting to avoid trouble, warned Frank that Sam was there and begged him to leave before anything happened. But Frank said if he left now he would look like a coward.

At the same time, one of Sam's friends left the bonfire and raced up the hill to warn Sam of Frank West's approach. One story is that Belle, upon hearing the warning, turned to Sam and muttered to him to confront their enemy.

This seems very unlikely, since Belle had worked so hard to keep Sam alive and out of trouble. But whatever she said or left unsaid was of little consequence. Sam was already out of the door and racing as noiseless as a shadow down the hill to the glowing fire.

When Sam saw Frank, he began scolding him bitterly for all of his betrayals. The two men started arguing, their voices rising louder with every breath. Twelve-year-old Dan Folsom heard the fury in their voices and was terrified. He started running up the hill for the shelter of the Surratt house, afraid of the gunfire he was sure would follow. He had gone a short ways when the first shot reverberated throughout the grove.

Sam had fired it. The bullet struck Frank with deadly force. He began to fall, but as he did he sent his own bullet flying. It crashed through Sam's body and on to graze Dan Folsom's cheek. Behind him, Sam staggered forward for some ten feet, and then he too fell dead.

The second dance was in progress when over the music and the clatter of the dancers' feet resounded the bursts of gunfire. Music and whirling dancers came to a sudden halt. In the silence, some of Sam's friends from the bonfire below burst into the room shouting that Sam and Frank had shot each other dead.

According to some witnesses, Belle's first reaction was a harsh order: "Why don't you bring 'em in and lay 'em out?" Others said that when the bodies were brought in, Belle rushed to her husband's side. Refusing to shed a single tear, her face drained white as a sheet as she knelt beside him and cradled his head in her arms. All the while she cursed the dead Frank West.

Chapter Thirteen

NEW MARRIAGE! NEW BABY!

It was a sad and uncertain Christmas for Belle and her family. Now that Sam was gone, his notorious friends who had been frequent visitors at the cabin scattered, leaving it free of outlaws for the first time in the seven years Sam and Belle had lived there.

But Belle also had a new and pressing problem. With Sam's death, she lost her citizenship in the Cherokee Nation and would have to give up her home and land. The thought of giving up this wilderness hideaway, which she loved, and starting all over again somewhere else was more than Belle could endure.

She solved her problem by inviting a twenty-four-year-old Creek, one of Tom Starr's adopted sons, to move in with her. His name was Jim July Starr. He was a good-looking young man, but without Sam's handsome chiseled features. He could speak English well, having attended elementary school. And he was also fluent in many of the territory's tribal tongues.

Belle's appearance was in sharp contrast to Jim July's youthful freshness. Hard outdoor life in the merciless Texas sun had darkened and thickened her once-soft olive complexion. The rounded oval of her face had lengthened and thinned. Her nose had taken on a sharp, chiseled edge, and her lips were set in two thin lines. Her once glossy black hair was harsh and brittle now, streaked here and there with iron gray strands. But her eyes, still sharp as a falcon's, looked out upon the world with a penetrating directness.

Despite Belle's worn appearance, she still possessed that aura of excitement that had attracted Sam and now fascinated Jim July. He had another reason, too, for accepting Belle's offer to move in with her. It would give him a house of his own and, as Belle's husband, a position of some standing. With everything decided, Jim July made the marriage official by announcing to all the Indian nations that he was moving in with Belle as husband and wife. That was all that was required to make a marriage legitimate according to tribal custom.

Eddie was upset about the marriage. The young Creek was only seven years older than himself. He did not want him for a stepfather. Belle tried to explain to her son that she had married Jim July for one reason only. There was no other way they could go on living in the place that the family had worked so hard to develop.

Pearl accepted the marriage more easily. She understood her mother's dilemma because she loved Youngers'

Bend, too, and did not want to see it lost to the family. Besides, she had a more pressing problem than Jim July: her coming baby.

Time was slipping by and she would have to make her move soon if she wanted to get away before her mother found out. She had already discussed her simple plan with Mabel. Pearl had some money of her own from fees she had received from the U.S. government as an informer at various trials. She could also raise a little more money by selling several horses she owned. According to her figures, the total would amount to some $200.

She told Mabel that her plan was to use the money to go someplace where she was unknown, have her baby and bring it up there, never again communicating with her mother. Mabel was doubtful. She told Pearl she did not believe she had nearly enough money to do all that. But Pearl just shrugged. It was her only option, she said.

Christmas and New Year's came and went, and still Pearl had not made a move. Now that the uncertain future was upon her, she continued drawing back, feeling timid, afraid of what her plan would bring. But before she did anything at all, the matter was taken out of her hands.

One evening an old family friend stopped by for a visit. He was Morris Kraft, a shopkeeper in Whitefield, where Belle had been doing most of her shopping. Kraft had had a long-time relationship with the Starr family, often providing bail or an alibi for one or another of them who was in trouble. He had always been especially fond of

Pearl, treating her as if she were his own granddaughter. Pearl still remembered the little red dress he had given her—the first red dress she had ever had, and which she loved.

When Kraft arrived that evening, Belle was alone in the cabin. She was in a playful mood. Pearl and Mabel were off on an errand, she told him, and she was preparing a prank for them when they returned. She was going to drape a sheet around her and greet the girls as a ghost, intoning a prophecy of doom in a low, sepulchral voice.

Kraft looked alarmed. He blurted out his concern. A ghost at such a time might do Pearl great harm, he said. Belle only laughed. When had her daughter ever been afraid of such a silly thing, she demanded. Why, Pearl would just laugh along with her.

Kraft gave Belle a piercing look, then asked her softly if she had failed to notice that her daughter was in a "delicate condition," a phrase used to describe pregnancy. Belle was horrified. She turned on Kraft in a white fury, demanding to know if he was the man who had seduced Pearl. Shocked at her accusation, the elderly shopkeeper told her bluntly that he was certainly not the culprit and indignantly left.

Belle fumed until the girls returned. Then she descended on Pearl, demanding to know the name of the man who had betrayed her. Pearl, taken by surprise, began stammering, then suddenly clamped her lips tight and said nothing. She knew that if her mother learned it was Bob McClure she might very well look for him and kill him on the spot. Pearl took her mother's flood of demands in silence, until finally she had had enough. Sobbing, she cried out that Belle could threaten her with death and she still would never reveal the man's name.

Finally, Belle gave up her fruitless grilling and began casting about for a solution to the problem. With this, Pearl felt it safe enough to tell her mother about a liveryman who, during her visits to Fort Smith, had persistently proposed marriage to her. Belle pounced on the information. With Pearl in tow, she set off for Fort Smith to pay a visit to the liveryman. He was much older than Pearl, but at least he was well-respected and wealthy: He owned a thriving livery rental service. Belle told him she had heard he had proposed to her daughter. There was, however, one obstacle. Pearl was pregnant. The liveryman, who still declared his undying love for Pearl, suggested that she see a doctor he knew who might agree to give Pearl an abortion, after which he promised to marry her. Belle thought it was a good idea, but Pearl rejected the offer.

An angry Belle then laid down a drastic ultimatum. If Pearl was determined to have the child, she would have to leave home to do so. And if she ever wanted to return, she could not bring the child with her because Belle never wanted to see it.

Pearl began packing her clothes. It was what she had planned to do in the first place. And now she had an idea where to go. Her grandmother Susan Reed had always loved her. Perhaps she would welcome her now. When Pearl was ready, she gave Mabel a tearful embrace and set off for Fort Smith.

At Fort Smith, Pearl stopped to thank the liveryman for his concern and to tell him she was leaving home forever. Once more he begged her to reconsider, pointing out there was another option. She could have the baby, place it in an orphanage, and then come back to marry him, her secret safe. But Pearl could not abandon the child, a last remembrance of her one true love. Taking leave of the liveryman, she boarded the train for Missouri. From the Missouri station, she had to ride horseback the thirty-five miles to Rich Hill. It was a wearing ride, and what if, after making it, she was turned away by her Grandmother Reed?

She had no need to worry. Grandmother Reed welcomed her with open arms. She told Pearl she was just on her way to Siloam Springs in Arkansas and asked if she would like to go along. Pearl accepted thankfully, and there on April 22, 1887, she gave birth to a little girl. Looking at the baby proudly, mother and great-grandmother both pronounced her the most beautiful baby in the world. Pearl named her after Aunt Mamie Reed, her father's sister.

The uncertain future Pearl had been dreading dissolved. With the backing of the loving Reed family, she was more resolved than ever to keep her child. She knew it was not going to be easy because she was well aware of how determined her mother always was to get her own way, either by force or by trickery. What Belle wanted most was to get Pearl back without the baby.

Pearl begged the family not to reveal her whereabouts to her mother, no matter how hard Belle pressed them. In the weeks ahead, Belle did try, firing off letter after letter demanding to know where Pearl was. The family always answered with the words Pearl had given them: She had left and they did not know where she had gone.

By the time little Mamie was a year old, the letters from Belle had become almost threatening. Put the child in an orphanage, put her up for adoption, get her out of Pearl's life. Pearl became fearful that her mother might spring a surprise visit on the Reeds to take care of matters herself. Pearl had to find a better hiding place than Rich Hill. And who better than her Aunt Mamie who lived in Wichita, Kansas? Belle had never met Aunt Mamie and did not even know where she lived.

Aunt Mamie welcomed Pearl and her little daughter with open arms. It looked as though Pearl had finally managed to outwit her mother. But when the child was about fifteen months old, Belle stepped in to change everything. She sent an urgent message to the Reed home in Rich Hill claiming that Eddie had been shot and was near death. He was calling for his sister. If Pearl wanted to see him alive, she had to hurry home at once. A twenty dollar bill was enclosed with the letter to help meet Pearl's travel expenses.

The Reeds forwarded the letter to Pearl. She read it over and over. Was it true? Was her brother close to dying? Or was this just another trick of her mother's to get her home? In the end, Pearl felt she could not take a chance. Begging her aunt to continue keeping the child's whereabouts a secret, she gave little Mamie a last kiss and hug, promising she would be back soon. Then she was off. It would be many years before Pearl would see her daughter again.

Chapter Fourteen

DANGER! DANGER!

When Pearl arrived at Youngers' Bend, she found that her brother really was near death. Belle told her that Jim July's no-good cousin, Mose Perryman, stole a mare from a rancher while Eddie was in his company. When Perryman was afraid he was about to be caught, he shot Eddie while the boy was sleeping, and then left him with the mare, making it look as though he were the thief. Fortunately, a neighboring rancher found Eddie in time and sent a message to Belle to get her wounded son.

Belle came and picked up Eddie, more dead than alive, and brought him home. She had been nursing him ever since. Pearl was shocked at the first sight of her brother. She could not leave him like this. She would stay until he was completely out of danger. Pearl lingered on, helping her mother nurse Eddie.

Pearl was surprised at how quiet everything was at home. The house was empty of all outlaws and fugitives from justice. The first to disappear had been Sam's outlaw friends, who after his death had never come back. Belle had made it plain to all her acquaintances that she would no longer offer shelter to outlaws fleeing from the law, even those who were former friends of hers. Belle showed Pearl the reason for this change, a letter she had received from Robert Owen, the U.S. Indian agent. The letter read:

> Madam:
>   The complaint against you for harboring bad characters has not, in my opinion, been established and is now dismissed.
>   I hope sincerely that you will faithfully carry out your promise to this office not to let such parties make your place a rendezvous.
>
>   Yours respectfully,
>   Robert L. Owen, United States Indian Agent

Belle explained that Owen had sent a copy of his letter to every newspaper in the Indian Territory so that they would know the truth and quit printing falsehoods about her.

Belle was very proud of that letter, which seemed to establish her at last as an upstanding citizen. And she had no intention of letting anyone's bad behavior drag her down. She had already warned Jim July and Eddie that if they got into any scrapes they would have to handle

Belle planted these trees around the schoolhouse at Youngers' Bend. *(Photo by Fred S. Barde, Fred S. Barde College. Courtesy of the Archives & Manuscripts Division of the Oklahoma Historical Society, 1464.3.)*

them on their own. She would no longer bail them out or hire lawyers for them.

Meanwhile, Eddie's wound was healing, and as his strength returned, Pearl began thinking of returning to her little girl. She wrote Aunt Mamie, telling her of her plans to pick up the child at Rich Hill and asking if she would take her there for the reunion.

Pearl expected to get a letter back from Aunt Mamie confirming her request. But as weeks passed without word from her aunt or the Reeds, Pearl began to feel that something was wrong. Was her mother intercepting her mail to find out where little Mamie was? Pearl became alarmed. Finally she asked Eddie, who was fully recovered now, to go to Whitefield and collect the mail next Thursday. That way she would know if there was anything for her in it.

Eddie would have done anything for his sister. On mail day, he rode to Whitefield and went into the store-post office. He told William S. Hall, the acting postmaster, that he had come to collect the mail. Hall informed him that he was under orders from Belle to give the mail only to her, and he refused to turn it over to Eddie. At this, Eddie drew his gun and pointed it at Hall, demanding the mail. Hall took one look at the business-like revolver and handed Eddie the mail. There was nothing in that batch for Pearl, so Eddie gave the lot to his mother.

Belle looked at him through narrowed eyes, then demanded that he go with her to the Whitefield post office. Facing Hall, Belle asked him why he had disobeyed her orders. Hall, not wanting to be on the wrong side of Belle, told her about Eddie and his gun.

With that, a grim-faced Belle pulled out her pistol and pointed it at Eddie, while with her free hand she grabbed a thick bull whip hanging on the wall of the store. She began thrashing Eddie's back and shoulders with it until he dripped with blood. Then she warned him never again to show such disrespect to Hall, a United States employee. Eddie, his back slashed with deep gashes from which the blood still dripped, glared back at her, eyes blazing with hatred, though he said nothing.

As Pearl treated the ugly gashes in Eddie's back, she realized that her mother's anger was fueled not only by Eddie's disrespect toward the postmaster, but for his interference with the mail. It confirmed Pearl's worst suspicions. Her mother had been confiscating any mail from the Reeds to find out where the child was so she could get rid of her for good, just as she had driven off Bob McClure. What Pearl did not know was that Belle had already intercepted Aunt Mamie's letter and had been firing off letter after letter of her own demanding the child be placed in an orphanage.

Finally, when Belle got no answers to her letters, she played her trump card. She threatened Mamie that if she refused to do as she was told, Belle would contact one of the gypsy gangs that was roaming around Missouri. She said she knew that for a fee the gypsies would kidnap the child and take her away forever. This terrified Aunt Mamie because the gypsies had the reputation of being cruel and sly. Thinking she was saving the little girl from a terrible fate, Aunt Mamie hurried the child off to an orphanage.

Belle had one more hurdle to cross to complete her campaign to get the child out of Pearl's life for good. One day, she showed her daughter a release form she had received from the orphanage. Pearl's signature would allow the orphanage to put the little girl up for adoption, and Belle demanded that Pearl sign it.

Pearl stared at the form before her. The weight of her mother's deceit hit her with full force. She gave a wild scream and yelled: "You can't make me sign this. You have done everything else to me, but you can't make me sign that paper." She shoved the paper away from her and ran out of the room.

When Pearl came back, the paper was gone and she assumed that her mother had given up and thrown it away. She consoled herself with the thought that though her mother had managed to put little Mamie in the orphanage, the child was safe as long as she did not sign the form. Meanwhile she felt she was needed at Youngers' Bend. The chaos in the cabin was escalating every day. There were frequent clashes between Eddie and his mother, between Jim July and Eddie, and even between Belle and Jim July. Pearl was the only buffer capable of keeping some kind of balance in the household.

But Pearl could not handle everything, and one day the tension erupted. Eddie wanted to attend a huge party in style. Dressed in his best, he asked his mother if he might borrow her favorite horse for the evening. Belle turned him down flat. But Eddie, as devious as his mother, waited until she had gone to bed to steal out of the house and down to the stables. He released the horse, mounted it, and rode off to the party, not returning until just before daybreak, when he stabled the horse and quietly slipped into his room.

He was sound asleep when Belle rose shortly after

dawn and went out to check the stables, as she did every morning. She found her favorite horse worn, grimy, and ungroomed. Belle snatched a riding whip from the stable wall and strode back to the house and into Eddie's room. She snatched the covers off the sleeping teenager and began lashing him with the whip.

Eddie fled the cabin and disappeared for two weeks. When he returned, the violent quarrels started again. Finally Eddie, in a frenzy of anger, shouted that he would kill her one day. Then he left the house for good, crossing the Canadian River and moving in with the Jackson Rowe family, who had a ranch on the other side.

With Eddie gone, Belle found herself short of hands to work the horses and the farm. She hired Mabel's brother Will, a steady young man and a good worker, to take Eddie's place. Now that Eddie was not around, the quarreling stopped. Pearl thought again of leaving, but still she lingered on, held by her mother's possessive grip. She decided she could stay through Christmas, New Year's, and even her mother's forty-first birthday on February 8, and her brother's eighteenth birthday on February 22.

Pearl found a new reason to stay when a visitor knocked on Belle's door one day in January. Belle found something vaguely threatening about him which she could not place. He was six feet tall with blue eyes that shone bright and hard in his seamed, sunburned face. His head was topped by bright orange hair.

The stranger introduced himself as Edgar Watson. He was, he said, a farmer from Arkansas who had been renting bottom land from a Mr. Hoyt, a rancher-farmer whose property was across the way in Choctaw territory. For some reason, the Choctaws did not like Watson and had refused him permission to extend his lease, so he was looking elsewhere. He had heard that Belle had some fine acreage for rent in Cherokee country. He was ready to pay a good fee for it. Belle was interested. Since Sam's death, she and Jim July had been unable to care for all their land and had been leasing out some of it to sharecroppers.

Though Belle had been suspicious of Watson at first, she had immediately taken a liking to his friendly wife. She was educated and cultured, not the kind of woman usually found on the frontier. And she was lonely and eager for friendship. She would make a wonderful neighbor, Belle told herself. It was this that swayed her in favor of the deal. Belle accepted the rental money and Watson prepared to move in.

As the friendship between Belle and Mrs. Watson grew, they began revealing intimate details of their past to each other. One day, in a moment of candor, Mrs. Watson unburdened herself of a dark secret about her husband that she had kept hidden from everyone. She told Belle they had not really come from Arkansas but from Florida, where they had fled because her husband was wanted for murder.

Belle received this information with horror. Though

she felt sorry for Mrs. Watson, she could not afford to have a murderer on her property—not after she had given her promise to Robert Owen, agent for the Indian Territory, who had written her the treasured letter. At the same time, she did not want to inform on the Watsons, especially as she was so fond of Mrs. Watson. She just wanted them off her property so she would not be accused again of sheltering outlaws if Watson's past were discovered. She told him that she had changed her mind and tried to give his money back to him. But Watson refused it.

Belle tried to work around Watson by approaching Joseph Tate, a recent arrival to the area. She asked him if he would like to sharecrop the land that Watson wanted. When Tate accepted the offer, Belle told Watson that she had to cancel her agreement to rent the land to him because she had already promised it to someone else, Joseph Tate. A determined Watson went to Tate and told him he would not get much peace if he sharecropped that particular parcel of bottom land. He painted a lurid picture of the swarms of sheriffs and their posses that were always roaming Youngers' Bend rounding up criminals. At any time, Belle might be arrested and even sent to jail for larceny, as had happened in the past. Then Tate himself could be in trouble, accused of aiding her. These stories so alarmed Tate that he backed out of the deal.

When Belle heard what Watson had done she cursed him roundly. Then in a low voice she added conspiratorially, "I don't suppose the United States officers would trouble you. But the Florida officers might."

Watson's face turned red. Without a word he turned and left. The deal was dead. But Pearl, listening to the conversation through the open door of the cabin, felt her skin crawl. She started scolding her mother for making such a dangerous enemy. But Belle only laughed. What could he do, a fugitive whose fate was in her hands? Perhaps he would leave now.

Pearl could only hope this would happen. But in January of 1889, she heard to her dismay that Watson was still around, living in a rented cabin on the Hoyt ranch where he had formerly farmed. The Hoyt ranch was just across the river from Youngers' Bend.

Chapter Fifteen

GUNFIRE AT SUNSET

The new year of 1889 promised a quiet and peaceful beginning for the Starr family. Eddie was no longer around to rile his mother. And to Belle's delight, Pearl was still at home. Things were more harmonious between Belle and her husband than they had been for a long while. On February 2, when Jim July had to go to Fort Smith to answer to an old charge of horse theft, Belle decided to keep him company part of the way.

The couple's first stop was at a little store where Belle often bought goods on credit. She now paid up her account, which amounted to some seventy-five dollars. Instead of turning back then, Belle decided to ride on a bit farther with Jim July. Toward sundown, they stopped at a friend's house where they spent the night. The next morning they parted. Jim July rode on to Fort Smith and his day in court, while Belle began retracing her way home.

At noon she revisited the little store. She was again

greeted by the owner and his wife, who invited her to lunch. Belle watered and fed her horse and then went inside for the meal. Both her host and hostess noticed how quiet, almost withdrawn, Belle was during the meal. Her concerned host asked her what was troubling her. She answered vaguely that things did not seem to have been going well with her lately. Then she blurted out that she was afraid for her life, that one of her enemies was going to kill her.

Her host had never seen her so apprehensive and unsure before. Taken by surprise, he was silent at first, and then he tried to cheer her up. "Thunder and lightnin' couldn't kill you," he exclaimed, laughing.

Belle made a wry face and seemed to change the subject by asking for scissors. Astonished at the request, her hostess jumped up and brought a pair. Belle, her old efficient self again, removed the large silk scarf she was wearing and cut it into two triangular pieces.

Belle handed one of the pieces to her hostess. It was to remember her by, she explained. Then, bidding host and hostess goodbye, she set out again for home. Around four in the afternoon she made her next stop, this time at the Rowe home where Eddie was living. Belle hoped to see her son there and perhaps smooth things over with him. But Eddie had just left to visit other friends, and Belle could only leave him a message.

Belle did not head for home immediately. Sunday afternoons were always pleasant times at the Rowe home because they liked to entertain. Many of the guests were the tenants who occupied the cluster of cabins on the Hoyt ranch next door. Among these guests, Belle spotted the burly form of Mr. Watson, who took one hard look at her and disappeared. She quickly put him out of her mind and went to visit an old friend, Mrs. Jerusha Barnes. The Barnes family was camped in the Rowe yard. Belle found Jerusha cooking dinner, and Belle knew that if she waited long enough she would be treated to some corn pone. Corn pone was Belle's favorite snack, and no one made sourdough corn pone like Jerusha Barnes.

Belle stayed a half hour, chatting with Jerusha while the corn pone baked. Then with a fresh, warm piece in her hand, she bade farewell to the Barnes and set off again, riding at a leisurely pace while munching the corn pone. The trail she followed ran along the outside of the fence that divided the Rowe ranch from the Hoyt ranch. Beyond the fence she could see the cluster of tenant cabins. Watson's was the nearest.

It was very late in the afternoon now. The sun hung on the horizon, throwing long black shadows across the land as Belle neared the corner of the fence. There the trail she followed intersected another trail that ran along the bank of the Canadian River. Turning down this trail, Belle would come to a ford. There she would cross the river and soon be back at Youngers' Bend.

Belle felt apprehension growing in her as she turned the fence corner and entered the river lane. She could not race her horse here because two days of heavy rains had turned the trail to mud. Because she had to focus her attention on the road to avoid the numerous potholes, she did not notice the dark shadow of a man crouched in the corner of the fence.

When Belle was just forty feet from the fence corner, the shadowy figure stood up boldly, leveled a two-barreled shotgun at Belle's back and fired. The blast broke the stillness. Belle fell from her horse into the muddy lane. The animal, panicked by the roar of the gun, rushed off into the twilight, heading for Youngers' Bend.

Belle was bleeding from her neck and side where a hail of buckshot had struck her. She struggled to get to her feet. But the figure was too fast for her. He leapt over the fence, and standing above her, emptied the other barrel of his gun into her face and shoulder, sending a second blast echoing across the countryside. This time Belle gave up her struggle and lay motionless in the mud. Satisfied, the murderer melted away into the twilight and disappeared.

Belle's riderless horse galloped on, coming to the ford where young Milo Hoyt had just crossed on his way home. He watched the horse plunge into the river and swim across it, scramble out and continue its dash for Youngers' Bend. Milo realized that something was terribly wrong and set off in the direction from which the horse had come.

Only a half mile away, Milo came upon Belle's body.

In the gathering twilight, he could not see the blood pooling around her, so he assumed she had been thrown by her horse. Leaving her, he galloped back to the ford to get Pearl, whom he found already there. Alarmed at seeing her mother's horse in the compound, its bridle askew, panting and wild-eyed, she had just ferried herself across the river.

After a quick exchange of words, Pearl mounted behind Milo and they set off at a brisk pace to the spot where Belle lay motionless. Milo left Pearl there while he raced off to get help from the nearest neighbor, a farmer named Alf White.

Pearl knelt in the mud beside her dying mother. In the thickening twilight she saw the dark pool of blood beneath Belle's body and knew she had been shot. But she was still alive. Pearl heard her mother's rasping breath. Tenderly, she cradled her bloody head in her arms, begging her to hang on, that help was coming.

Belle could not answer. She gave a last gasping breath, which faded away, and then she was gone. Bewildered, Pearl continued to crouch there, cradling her mother's head while the twilight darkened around them.

Chapter Sixteen

THE FUNERAL

When Milo appeared at the door of the White house, he found the family already very uneasy. Mrs. White had been home alone when she heard the shots. She went to the door to see a horse with a sidesaddle still in place galloping for the ford. When her husband arrived home shortly afterwards, his wife told him what she had seen. He was about to go to investigate when Milo appeared and told them Belle had been in a bad accident.

White and Milo went off to ask another neighbor, Charles Acton, to bring his wagon for Belle. When the three men drove the wagon to the site where Belle's body lay, they found Pearl kneeling at her mother's side. The two men lifted Belle and put her body in the wagon. Then Acton drove back to the White house where they laid Belle's body on a bed. By this time, they could see plainly that she had been shot. All night, Acton and Pearl sat beside the still form, a lonely wake, joined quietly now and then by others.

Before daybreak, Acton left Belle's side to go to the nearest telegraph office and send a telegram to Jim July telling him that his wife had been murdered. Meanwhile, word had been getting around fast, and the White house was filling up with neighbors.

One of the first to arrive was Eddie, who had not seen his mother for two months. During that time, his feelings of resentment had cooled. He now gave way to feelings of loss and guilt. If he had not left the Rowe house when he did, he would have been there to see his mother. He could even have been with her on that lonely ride home. Then the killer would not have dared to strike. The least he could do now was to use the tracing skills he had learned from Sam to find his mother's killer. He and a companion went to the spot where Belle had died. Numerous footprints surrounded the dark patch of blood. But only one set, the clear imprints of a large boot size, led to the body and away again in different directions. Eddie followed the prints back through the field to the fence corner. There he found the ground had been trampled. He guessed this must have been the spot where the assailant had hidden.

Eddie went back to the lane and then began to follow the same prints that led away from the body in the opposite direction, until they entered a nearby stand of trees. Here they meandered aimlessly. But Eddie supposed the killer was just trying to walk on the patchwork cover of leaves beneath the trees to hide his tracks. Here he lost the trail. But he learned from another tracker—Turner England—who had come earlier, that he had been able to follow the telltale trail that led through the woods to within 150 yards of Watson's cabin, but standing there he had felt a deadly chill of fear and had quickly turned back.

Meanwhile Jim July, who was preparing for his trial at Fort Smith, received the telegram. Those who saw him at that moment were struck by the fierce glare in his black eyes. He saddled his horse, snatched up a bottle of whiskey, and ignoring his upcoming court appearance, was off like the wind, shouting that someone was going to pay for this.

Late Monday night, Jim July reached the cabin at Youngers' Bend. He had covered the distance from Fort Smith in record time. Belle's body had already been brought to the cabin. Jim July went into the room where his wife had been laid out and stood quietly looking down at her. Then he turned from her and began firing off questions. Finally, he drew Eddie aside for a private conversation, the two young men brought closer together in grief than they ever had been before.

Eddie told Jim July about the tracks made by a larger than normal boot, the kind Watson wore, and how those tracks led back to within a short distance of the Watson cabin. Jim July nodded grimly. He knew of the bitter disagreement Belle had had with Watson over her land. Though she had not told him about Watson's dark past in Florida, he knew from the Choctaws that Watson had a reputation for violence. Sooner or later, Jim July told himself, he would have the truth out of the man.

Tuesday was a sad day for the Starrs. Out on the rocky ledge that skirted Belle's small lawn and her carefully tended flower beds, several husky men were digging her a grave that would overlook this nook of wilderness she had loved so much. Inside the cabin, the women were working over Belle's body. They bathed her, then rubbed her skin with a turpentine and cinnamon oil mixture. They dressed Belle in her finest black velvet riding habit, the one she always wore to dances or important events. As the women finished their work, the coffin arrived. John Cates, a carpenter, had fashioned it out of pine wood. The women lined it with a fine black cloth fringed with white lace.

When all was ready, they laid Belle's body in it, crossing her arms on her breast. One of the women brought out Belle's favorite revolver and placed it in her right hand, bending her stiff fingers over it. Everything was ready now for the burial that would take place the next day.

Word of the coming funeral traveled fast. Men and women from every tribe were there—Choctaws, Creeks, and most prominently, Cherokees, including the Starrs' extended family. Belle was well-liked and respected by all of them. There were also a number of white sharecroppers. Most of the women who had come were showing their grief openly, for they remembered the many times Belle had been there for them and their children.

Outlaws, whom in the past Belle had sheltered, were there to pay their respects. Among the crowd there were also men who had felt the lash of Belle's whip or her tongue. They had come, though reluctantly, afraid their absence might point to their guilt, since they had been heard making angry threats against her.

Jim July's gaze drifted across the crowd of mourners until it came to rest on Watson and his wife, standing in the background. The couple acted very nervous. Jim July's accusing stare never left Watson's face as the funeral began. It would be a short service. No minister was there to perform the usual Christian rites. None of the dirges chanted at Cherokee burials were heard. The congregation stood in stony silence as grim-faced pallbearers carried the pine coffin through the open door of the cabin. Down the steps and across the handkerchief lawn the pallbearers trod solemnly to the shelf where the grave had been dug. They set the coffin down beside the open grave, removed the lid, and stepped back.

One by one, the crowd began filing by the open coffin. The Cherokees, who had always been closest to Belle, had brought one last gift for her. Following an ancient custom, each Cherokee dropped a small piece of corn pone into the coffin, the corn pone Belle had so loved in life.

Eddie and Pearl were the last to stand beside the coffin.

In deference to them, the crowd waited silently while Belle's children bade their mother a last farewell. Finally, the two stepped back and the pallbearers came forward. They replaced the lid and nailed it down. Then they lifted the coffin and lowered it into the grave.

The gravediggers began shoveling dirt and stony debris into the open grave. Shovelful after shovelful rained on the coffin until the work was done. Now a lonely mound marked the spot where Belle Starr lay silent.

People were turning to go when, like a bird of prey, Jim July streaked through the crowd and stopped in front of Watson and his wife, who were trying to hurry off. Jim July, his face dark with fury, was holding his Winchester rifle, trained on Watson. In a loud voice, the Cherokee accused Watson of murdering his wife.

Watson acted quickly. His glittering blue eyes stared back calmly at Jim July. Then in one move, he reached out and grabbed the arm of Cates, who was standing next to him, and pushed his hostage between himself and Jim July's gun. The pinioned man realized that a single blast of that gun would not only kill him, but would be the signal for a terrible gun fight. He shouted to Watson to put up his hands and surrender, and do it at once.

Watson let go of Cate's arm and raised both hands. He spoke again, telling Jim July that if he killed him he would be killing the wrong man. Then he begged the assembled crowd not to leave him alone with the hot-headed Jim July.

Jack Rowe stepped forward and, along with another couple and Mrs. Watson, offered to spend the night at the Starr cabin to protect Watson. In the morning, they would see that he got to Fort Smith for a proper trial. Jim July and Watson reluctantly agreed to this, and the crowd finally dispersed.

That night must have been an uneasy one for Watson. It could not have been much better for him the following day, when Jim July, Eddie, and Jack Rowe set off for Fort Smith. During the long trek that lay ahead, Watson had only Rowe to protect him from being killed along the way.

Chapter Seventeen

THE KILLER EXPOSED

Once the group arrived at Fort Smith, Jim July took his prisoner to United States Commissioner Stephen Wheeler and swore out a complaint against him, stating that he had murdered Belle Starr and presenting a long list of witnesses who could testify to the fact, including Eddie and Pearl Starr. After hearing Jim July's accusation, Commissioner Wheeler told Watson the accusation was so serious he would have to post bail immediately, and when he was unable to do so, he was jailed.

Watson may have even felt relieved to be in jail, safe from Jim July's smoldering fury. Despite his anger, Jim July had been taught in school that he could rely on the laws of the United States to mete out justice. So he made no objection, trusting the outcome to the slow legal process.

During his stay in jail, Watson hired a well-known attorney, William M. Mellette, to represent him. Then, coached by his lawyer, he began spinning a web of lies.

He painted himself as a simple bewildered farmer unable to understand why he should be thought a murderer. He had had no trouble with anyone since his arrival a year ago to raise a crop on leased Choctaw land. He hardly knew Belle Starr and certainly had never quarreled with her. He could not think of any reason at all "to even feel hard toward her."

To every accusation Jim July's witnesses brought against him, Watson had a ready answer. For example, the prints of a large-sized boot had been traced coming and going from the crime scene. Yes, he wore that size, but a lot of other men did too. But most important, where was the motive?

Pearl could have supplied the missing motive, but she was too terrified to describe the incriminating conversation she had heard between Watson and her mother a short while before Belle was killed. What if Judge Parker dismissed her information as mere hearsay and released Watson? Would Watson then come after her? Pearl testified that she knew her mother was mad at Watson without saying why.

This made it possible for Watson to counter Pearl's testimony with a puzzled frown and his meek assertion that if Belle was really angry with him he could not imagine why. So far as he knew, there had never been a cross word between them. His remarks seemed plausible. There was only one bit of strong evidence that was very hard to explain away—the nicks found in the gun shells scattered around Belle's body. Those telltale nicks pointed directly at Watson, since they proved that the murder weapon was one of Watson's guns.

But Watson's clever lawyer was even able to explain away that solid proof of the defendant's guilt. The lawyer pointed out that although the shells had come from Watson's gun, there was no proof that Watson had fired the gun. As he explained to Commissioner James Brizzolara, who was now handling the case, Watson seldom locked his door. Anyone could have slipped inside, borrowed the gun and then returned it to frame Watson. And who more likely than Jim July, who had been heard at times complaining bitterly about his wife? Couldn't he have sneaked back from Fort Smith to use the gun to kill Belle Starr and then have blamed Watson for it?

In the end, the lawyer convinced Brizzolara that all the evidence was circumstantial. There was no real proof of Watson's guilt. And there were a lot of other people around who had a greater motive to kill Belle Starr.

Commissioner Brizzolara agreed and ordered Watson released at once. Without wasting any time, Watson and his wife packed hurriedly and, traveling through Arkansas, made their way back to Florida. When Jim July heard of Watson's release, he felt betrayed by the very laws in which he had placed his trust. He left Youngers' Bend and never returned. Instead, he drifted through Indian Territory, finally joining up with a gang in the Chickasaw

Nation. He did intend, however, to return to Fort Smith for his trial and was making plans to renew his bail and ask for a new court date.

Before Jim July could carry out his plans, a posse led by a man named Bob Hutchins surprised him. Without giving Jim July a chance to surrender, Hutchins shot him in the back. Then, concerned over his own illegal act, he brought the mortally wounded Cherokee to the Fort Smith prison hospital. Jim July died there without making any kind of confession. But a rumor quickly spread that in the last minutes of his life he had murmured, "I killed Belle Starr."

Nobody who lived in the area around Youngers' Bend believed the rumor. Jim July had never shown any violence. So far as anyone knew, he had never killed anybody before. And his chief grievance against Belle was an insignificant one: He had often been heard to grumble about the way she treated him like a child instead of a husband.

Meanwhile, the Council of the Cherokee Nation acted quickly. Three weeks after Jim July's death, it disposed of the Starr holdings. The land itself went back to the Cherokee Nation, but the improvements on it could be claimed only by a rightful inheritor. Belle had left no written will. But witnesses came forward to swear she had told them that in case of her death all improvements were to go to Jim July. This was accepted by the Cherokee courts, and now that Jim July had died without heirs, all improvements along with the land were turned over to the Cherokee Nation, leaving Pearl and Eddie almost penniless.

By this time, all kinds of rumors were swirling around, each one centering on a different suspect now that Watson had been released. One suggested the culprit was Tom Starr, who had remained angry with Belle for encouraging Sam to go after Frank West. But this rumor died quickly. Tom Starr had just recently been released from prison, a tired old man with broken health. How could he find the strength to build a raft of logs, pole it across the turbulent river, ambush and shoot Belle, and then return the same way he had come?

Other rumors named various cowpokes and ranchers who had exchanged harsh words with Belle, often reinforced by a stinging flick of her riding quirt. More than one of these suspects had been heard uttering death threats against her.

And then there was Eddie, who had suffered most from his mother's brutal beatings. He had often been heard repeating his baleful threat, "I hate her. I will kill her one day." Some even mentioned Pearl, angry because her mother robbed her of her child.

It was not until 1910 that the true killer of Belle Starr was identified by Florida lawmen. That was the day a posse finally gunned down Watson during a fierce shootout. A Tampa, Florida, newspaper heralded his death with a front page story that began, "Edgar A.

Watson, outlaw and slayer of Belle Starr . . ." In the twenty-one years following his murder of Belle Starr, Watson had killed at least thirteen more people in the state of Florida alone.

Several years later, Pearl commissioned workers to build a two-foot-high stone wall around Belle's grave. She had a limestone slab roof laid over the walls, forming a rustic vault. Pearl then selected a block of marble for the headstone and hired a local stonecutter named Joseph Dailey to engrave it with the symbols that had played a prominent part in Belle's life. One was a bas-relief of Belle's favorite mare, and with it a star and a bell. Beneath these, the stonecutter engraved:

BELLE STARR
Born in Carthage, Mo.
Feb. 5, 1848
DIED
Feb. 3, 1889
Weep not for her the bitter tears.
Nor give the heart to vain regret;
Tis but the casket that lies here
The gem that filled it sparkles yet,

Conclusion

In July following Belle's death, Eddie was tried for horse theft, and Judge Parker gave him an unusually stiff sentence—seven years in the state penitentiary at Columbus, Ohio. With her brother gone, Pearl felt more alone than she had ever felt before. When Will Harrison (Mabel's brother) proposed to her she quickly accepted, perhaps because she felt that a stable home might help her get her daughter back. She contacted her Aunt Mamie and learned that her child had already been put up for adoption and could not be returned.

With her hopes gone, Pearl fell into a deep depression. She became moody and quarrelsome. She and her husband began to berate each other until Pearl left home. She began drifting through Arkansas homeless and almost penniless. Without any skills she finally took up the only profession open to her. She entered a "boarding house for girls," as brothels were called, and became a prostitute.

Pearl was attractive and cultured, and her pleasing

soft-spoken personality made her a favorite among the visitors to the boarding house. Money began rolling in. It was with some of this money that Pearl restored the neglected grave of her mother, for whom she felt a strange mixture of love and devotion despite the nagging sense of betrayal she still suffered.

Pearl's other objective was to release her brother from prison. After three years she was able to obtain a pardon for him, and Eddie was soon on his way home. He was aghast to find Pearl in Fort Smith, now a Madam in her own sumptuous boarding house for girls. Telling her he would rather have stayed in prison than to see her like this, he left abruptly never to see his sister again. He took a job as a railroad guard, married a pretty Cherokee school teacher, and settled down in Indian Territory. But in less than three years, he was fatally shot by a pair of liquor smugglers while he was attempting to arrest them.

Pearl continued her successful career as a Madam. She reportedly married two or three more times and had two more daughters. She became a celebrity of sorts in Fort Smith, earning the respect of local merchants and civic leaders for her honesty in business dealings.

However, times were changing. In 1907, Oklahoma was granted statehood and the formerly protected Indian Territory occupied by the Five Civilized Tribes was opened to the public. Farmers, ranchers, and criminals of various sorts all began flooding in.

Frontier cities and towns were becoming tamed as men

Pearl (far right) pictured with two of the women who lived at her "boarding house for girls."

brought their families to live with them. Churches and schools sprang up. Women's organizations, including the Women's Christian Temperance Union, began actively campaigning to clean up the frontier of such activities as drinking and prostitution. In Fort Smith, the reformers' chief target was Pearl's fancy brothel. By 1916, a city bill was passed that made prostitution illegal. It was time for Pearl to go.

During her stay in Fort Smith, Pearl had been shrewdly purchasing the best real estate in town. Now she sold everything and moved to Bisbee, Arizona, where she opened the Starr Hotel and bought an interest in a copper mining company. Now she had one objective—to find her daughter Mamie.

Once more, Pearl wrote to the orphanage where her mother had sent Mamie. To her surprise, she received a return letter from her lost daughter whose adoptive parents had changed her name to Flossie Pearl. They had died recently and Pearl's letter had been forwarded to Flossie.

That letter brought mother and daughter together. They corresponded by letter until 1924 when Flossie came for a final reunion, bringing along her teenage son. Pearl was touched to learn that, although Flossie and her husband Charlie had known nothing about Flossie's biological father, they had still given their son Robert's name.

Flossie's visit came just in time. The following year, Pearl died of a stroke at the age of fifty-seven. Her daughters gathered in Arizona to bury her in a sun-streaked cemetery, far from the dark tangled wilderness that held the grave of her mother, whose possessive love had once ruled and ruined her daughter's life with its magnetic force. That force has caused some in modern times to name Belle Starr one of America's earliest feminists, who vigorously defended her right to equality as a woman in a male-dominated world.

Appendix

THE MAKING OF A LEGEND

The late nineteenth century was a time of immense technological development. Recent improvements in printing and paper manufacturing had reduced the cost of publishing. Expanded educational opportunities also increased literacy levels. More people could now enjoy reading. Soon a new industry developed that produced magazines and inexpensive novels for the average reader. This development coincided with the post-Civil War settling of the Western frontier. What better subject for the new genre than the wild tales of outlaws who lived on the edges of civilization? It is because of these changes that the tales of the West became, in many respects, America's core mythology. The facts were less important than the tale. This mythological approach to the characters and stories of the West continued into the twentieth century and formed the basis of the movie western.

Belle Star was the perfect subject to fill the needs of this proliferating industry centered on the Old West. Her friendship with such famous outlaws as the James brothers and the Youngers, and her marriages to outlaws Jim Reed and Sam Starr, made it easy for writers to transform Belle into the Bandit Queen of an outlaw band of her very own.

Although Belle delighted in excitement and the company of outlaws, she was also intensely proud of her old and respected family name and fiercely guarded its reputation. Despite her efforts, she continued to gather some notoriety in parts of Texas, Arkansas, and the Indian Territory, though she was scarcely known elsewhere.

Worldwide fame came to Belle only after her death. It began with a brief obituary sent by the Fort Smith newspaper, *The Elevator*, to kindred newspaper offices in the big Eastern cities. Most of the newspapers ignored the obscure item. Only the *New York Times* honored it with a headline that read: "A Desperate Woman Killed."

In part, the story ran:

> Belle was the wife of Cole Younger . . . Jim Starr [sic] her second husband was shot down by the side of Belle less than two years ago . . . Belle Starr . . . married Cole Younger directly after the war, but left him and joined a band of outlaws that operated in the Indian Territory. She had been arrested for murder and robbery a score of times but always managed to escape.

Linking Belle's name to Cole Younger's sprang from an innocent remark Belle made during one of her rare interactions with reporters, whom she usually tried to avoid. She said she had fallen in love with "a dashing young guerrilla" when she was less than fifteen years old and had married him. Marriage records show that the young man could only have been Jim Reed, but some eager newshound preferred to interpret the remark as referring to Cole Younger, who had been a visitor at the Shirley home. This rumor persisted despite denials from both Belle and Cole.

The item in the *New York Times* caught the attention of Richard K. Fox, editor and publisher of the sensational tabloid, the *National Police Gazette*. Always hungry for notorious stories, Fox was intrigued by the brief news item. By the end of 1889, he had produced a paperback titled *Belle Starr, the Bandit Queen or the Female Jesse James*. The book, spun mostly from Fox's vivid imaginiation, sold for twenty-five cents a copy and was snapped up by thousands of readers worldwide. Belle Starr instantly became a legendary figure of the mysterious Wild West.

A spate of writers rushed to capitalize and expand on the sensational story, enlarging it with their own fictional spin. Belle was so popular that she became the subject of plays, songs, and poems. William Harmon devoted an entire chapter to Belle in his 1898 book, *Hell on the Border*, which tells the story of Hanging Judge Parker.

Harman, who was a native of Arkansas, relied heavily on the fictional information in Richard K. Fox's book, instead of researching primary sources.

The final travesties occured decades later. Burton Rascoe's biography of Belle Starr, *The Bandit Queen*, was published in 1941. This book went even further in sensationalizing Belle's life. In the same year, Belle was portrayed on the silver screen in a highly sanitized and totally false movie version of her life starring Gene Tierney. Belle was depicted as a beautiful young girl tricked into criminal acts by cruel Southern aristocrats. Another film cast her as a concerned woman trying to convince other outlaws to mend their evil ways.

It was not until the 1980s that scholars attempted to clear Belle's name. Joseph Steele, author of *Starr Tracks: Belle and Pearl Starr*, interviewed the women's descendants and was given access to old letters, marriage records, and pictures from family albums to bring the truth about the Starr family to light.

The well-known Old West historian, Glenn Shirley, (no relation to Belle) researched court house archives, historical museums, libraries, newspaper records, and interviews to help lay to rest the old myths about Belle in his book *Belle Starr and Her Times*.

Bibliography

BOOKS

Florin, Lambert. *Western Wagon Wheels*. Seattle, WA: Superior Publishing Co., 1970.

Foote, Shelby. *The Civil War—Secession to Fort Henry*. Alexandria, VA: Time-Life Books, 1999.

Foreman, Grant. *The Five Civilized Tribes*. Norman, OK: University of Oklahoma Press, 1834.

Fox, Richard K. (editor) *Belle Starr, the Bandit Queen, or the Female Jesse James*. New York: Richard K. Fox, Publisher, 1889.

Harman, Samuel W. *Hell on the Border: He Hanged Eighty-eight Men*. Fort Smith, AR: Phoenix Publishing Co., 1898.

Lackmann, Ron. *Women of the Western Frontier in Fact, Fiction and Film.* Jefferson, NC: McFarland and Company, Inc., Publishers, 1997.

McReynolds. Edwin C., *Missouri: A History of the Crossroads State.* Norman, OK: University of Oklahoma Press, 1962.

Moody, Ralph. *Stagecoach West.* New York: Thomas Crowell, Publisher, 1964.

Nevin, David. *The Expressmen.* New York: Time-Life Books, 1974.
———. *The Texans.* New York: Time-Life Books, 1975.

Rascoe, Burton. *Belle Starr: The Bandit Queen.* New York: Random House, 1941.

Reed, Marjorie, (illustrator) and James S. Copley (author). *The Colorful Butterfield Overland Stage.* Palm Desert, CA: Best West Publishers, 1966.

Seagraves, Anne. *Soiled Doves.* Hayden, ID: Wesanne Publishers, 1994.

Shirley, Glenn. *Belle Starr and Her Times.* Norman, OK: University of Oklahoma Press, 1982.

Steele, Phillip W. *Starr Tracks: Belle and Pearl Starr*. Gretna, LA: Pelican Books, 1989.

Trachtman, Paul. *The Gunfighters*. New York: Time-Life Books, 1974.

MAGAZINE ARTICLES

Arnott, Richard D., "Bandit Queen, Belle Starr." *Wild West*, Leesburg, VA, August 1997.

Moulton, Candy (Interviewer). "Phillip Steele Also Tracks the Starrs, Belle and Pearl." *Wild West*, Leesburg, VA, August 1997.

Norman, Geoffrey. "The Cherokee." *National Geographic,* Washington, D. C., May 1995.

Wilson, Lori Lee. "Although Born to One of the Wild West's Most Notorious Couples, Ed Reed Made Good in the End." *Wild West*, Leesburg, VA, August 1997.

Index